INSPIRATIONAL POEMS OF THE 21st CENTURY

REV. HAROLD E. B. JOHN

ISBN: 978-1-963565-89-8 (Paperback)
ISBN: 978-1-967375-04-2 (E-book)

Library of Congress Control Number: 2025909360

Printed in the United States of America

Published by:

info@thequippyquill.com
(302) 295-2278

Table of Contents

Inspiration Poems Of The 21st Century

LOVE POEM TO MY QUEEN

AFFILIATED QUOTE:

"Love comes from in within, from in within it stays; from in within, it is expressed to its host. With that love, all is conquered"

Love Poem to My Queen

Our love is great and fashioned by divine expertise;
Steadfastly I hold you in my heart and perpetually stay our love;
Though far apart, together we stay.
True love survives all obstacles and enough to withstand a tornado.
Deep inside, I will always love you while I live.
Deep inside, I will always love you even when I die.
Deep inside, I will always love you in eternity.

Love, is the song I sing to you.
Love is what I bring to the table and submit to you;
Love is always dreaming and fantasizing about you and me in Paradise;
Extend your love to me while I live;
Love me little, love me more, and love me forever.
The beautiful spring flowers you are as I am saturated with your love;
My senses are mesmerized and hypnotized by that special aroma;
My heart clings, my whole body shivers with ecstasy and feeling so
pleasurable.
Love, is the song I sing to you.

My love for you is pure, true, priceless, and not for sale is the sign.
My love is faithful, trustworthy, compassionate, enduring, and caring;
Constant and active stays my love forever.
My love generates assurance, sealing my concerns for you.
You are my Queen, my African Queen.
The thoughts of you console my soul;
To hold you close to me is my intention.
Love, is the song I sing to you.

True endeavor is generated from your love;
Extreme hot and strong is that love;
With my heart, I sing to you;
With my love, I pray for you.
Within me, every minute I long to hold you if I can.
Whatever separates us must be destroyed.
Love me daily, love me stronger.
Love, is the song I sing to you.

POEM TO MY QUEEN

<u>AFFILIATED QUOTE:</u>

"The Queen of my heart, the precious one; all day long cleanses become my heart; so be my attitude with the ruddy drops expelled through her mind".

Poem to My Queen

Love is giving, forgiving, taking, and partaking;
You are the sweetest joy, most comforting reassurance;
Your presence sends trills through my central system;
Your wonders travel through me in the span of a second;
Your love makes me feel at home no matter where I am;
Our love stamps assurance of a companion always by my side.

Love is amazing, beautiful, and precious;
You are true, real, trustworthy, and dependable;
Your commitment has formed an unbreakable bond between us;
You are implanted in the deepest part of my heart;
Your love sneaks out as often to put a smile on my face;
Our love is serenity in our soul, a quiet gratitude in our lives.

Love endures and brings happiness between us;
You are the sweetest aroma that follows me everywhere;
Your presence after ninety-two days works miracle within me;
You are my African Queen with a glow that energizes me;
Your love for me gives me hope in my darkest circumstances;
Our love is divine; forever, we live; forever, we stay.

Love strengthens and conquers all with peace of all;
You are the symbol of peace within me;
All that I need is to be with my Queen;
To gaze at the beautiful spring face glowing all over;
My heart waits for that day of freedom and liberty;
Our love will never die; our joy dominates forever.

POEM TO MY WIFE

AFFILIATED QUOTE:

"A wife so sweet
A wife so beautiful;
A wife so considerate,
A wife so compassionate,
A wife, a partner, a team player,
A friend you are so loving and so dear to me".

Poem to My Wife

My wife, my Queen, my beautiful African Queen;
The precious mineral that engulfs my soul;
A day without her is a thousand-pound weight on me;
My joy, happiness, and concentration,
Increase just by the thought of her.
Precious mineral is gracious, loving, and compassionate;
I seek her presence to smell her sweet aroma;
My Queen, my beautiful African Queen, come to me.

My wife, my Queen, my beautiful African Queen;
My love for you is priceless, supersedes the highest mountain;
I seek no other. You fulfill all my ecstasy;
In a corrupt world, staying faithful,
Precious mineral remains;
Your love is solid as a mountain and smooth as spring water.
Two in one united we are in ways, thinking, likes, and dislikes;
My queen, my beautiful African Queen, come to me.

My wife, my Queen, my beautiful African Queen;
Higher power, bring my precious mineral to me,
To taste the juicy tongue; feel the well-fashioned body;
My life encompasses mysteries.
Precious minerals fulfill that mystery.
I look all over; I see none as beautiful as my precious mineral;
Custom-made to my liking, so is precious mineral to me;
My Queen, my beautiful African Queen, come to me.

My wife, my Queen, my beautiful African Queen;
Oh precious, what will I do without your love?
Precious mineral stays trustworthy and faithful to me;
In times of disappointment,
Our covenant we utilize for comfort,
All will be well precious; negative occurrences are temporal;
Let's picture our future together in prosperity and abundance;
My Queen, my beautiful African Queen, come to me.

My wife, my Queen, my beautiful African Queen;
For your eyes are so modestly beaming from within;
I stand at the door of my precious mineral's soul;
As God's star, truthful she becomes;
With the garment of God, she walks.
The very strangest and sudden thing;
Is surprise to all that my Queen stays with me.
My Queen, my beautiful African Queen, come to me.

A WIFE SO STRONG

AFFILIATED QUOTE:

"With all the trials, tribulations, and calamities, falter not she remains. As a solid rock, so she stands".

A Wife So Strong

A wife so strong, so determined to overcome;
We shower each other with Babe, Mama, Papa, and African Queen.
A glorious way, expressing unique exciting feelings;
There is no other better than what we share;
We are not together to play,
Not drifting, not procrastinating.
Struggle is unable to break us; with God's help, we face it.
In God's name, let us be brave, stand up, and hold fast;
We are strong together, united we fight.

A wife so strong, so determined to overcome;
The sweet words shared enhance our memory.
Roses and nourishment we keep, casting out thorns of spoil;
The days of evil encompass us,
Aware we are of the enemies;
Fighting hard they're determined to set us apart.
United and coordinated become our perceptions and perspectives,
But our love stands supreme over their charms;
We are strong together, united we stand.

A wife so strong, so determined to overcome;
A light of immortal beauty proudly covers her face;
She moves with the glow of light that reminds me, she is mine.
The smiles that mesmerize, her chocolate tint that glows;
Pleasurable, exciting, and good days
I am reminded that set peace in me.
A woman so compassionate with action that keeps me centered.
The love that no other can experience except me;
We are strong together, united we stand.

A wife so strong, so determined to overcome;
She talks softly, observes attentively, expresses feelings openly;
Hidden from all, I feel her presence all over me;
A glance reveals the dark and bright aspects of her eyes;
She watches every move and puts me in place;
My perfume departs, her fragrance
Upholds me with that sexy stride;
With delightful hugs and kisses, young again I become;
We are strong together, united we stand.

A wife so strong, so determined to overcome;
In the cage, serving time, thinking of the next visit;
For that presence to thrill and lighten my inner core;
United as one flower vase in the Book of Life with overwhelming love;
Always reminded of the partnership,
Friendship and romance we share;
Generate endurance in strength, hope, and patience;
Our strong love, faith, and confidence will never fade;
We are strong together, united we stand.

GAINING CHARISMA

AFFILIATED QUOTE:

"So stays the inner determination, so stays the inner restraint; though burdensome in every angle, progressively the move becomes as endurance and strength to continue is gained".

Gaining Charisma

If I knew when I was a teenager;
I would have stated "God knows the best";
Now Lord, help me to find you in my moment of darkness;
Turning myself over I did, to the care of God Almighty;
The choice was made, spirituality is my path.
Assigned angels rejuvenate my attitude,
Generating growth and change within;
Deeply my belief increases as my quest
In religious and spiritual sects are developed.
Highly I held my face, to the Pure White Light Spirits.
Though for a moment I am lost, I do not see, nor realize;
Hopefully, I wait to experience salvation and prosperity;
It is just a moment away, I can feel it, I can sense it;
God is at work, with my significant other. I feel great; I will grab it.
God's plan is like lilies; pure, white, and mysterious;
For each mystery, a key is available to unfold;
Praise God from whom all blessings flow.

If I knew when I was a teenager;
I would have surrendered and humble to the Lord.
Now confident, I get ready for the hard times;
It's really strange sometimes, no one understands.
For a moment, my universe is chaotic.
Darkness dominates, and everything seems to be wrong.
The sweet voice of African Queen exclaimed
"Hold on Papa, you can do it, you are strong, Wait on the Lord".
Consoling smile overwhelmed me as
African Queen speaks bravely and truly;
I realized my life is united with a trustworthy partner;
A silvery laugh ripples through my enlightened face.
There's health, strength, and goodness in the mirth;
The destiny of plentiful and prosperity will be fulfilled.
God is at work; goals are achieved just by a simple command;
Praise God for melting, molding, filling, and using me.

BE COURAGEOUS

<u>**AFFILIATED QUOTE:**</u>

"Sat on his faded cheek in pluck, ascending he stays, implied it is what is needed, in spite of fear. Word of God is read, prayer and meditation are done, and ways to serve others are done. With God's guidance, fearlessly he stays".

Be Courageous

Seeking courage increases boldness
With God's salvation;
I dare nothing, facing nothing,
Need nothing, expect nothing;
Seeking the courage to face what I cannot change;
To stay the course, though human,
Though tough, divinity is needed.
Maybe, I have to push a little, push with
More effort, maybe, push bigger.
Life is my choice, bravery is within me.
For my deeds, to love and applaud
as African Queen taught me.
"I am with you; you have a friend with you";
The voice echoes.
Praying I did for endurance and strength.
Trying to reach me,
My Spirits Band is at work.
The negative attitudes I discerned.
With courage and determination, I eliminated them.
Praying daily becomes a daily routine.
As I kneel, seeking mercy,
I see the glow of God.
"Endure in hope and patience", says the Lord.
Being obedient, humble, and submissive is the answer.
I Jumped with excitement and confidence,
I moved to face the challenges.
God is available at the doorstep; Search and you will find him.

Seeking courage, old ways washed away,
Attitude changed; I am rejuvenated.
I dare something, face something,
Need something, expect something.
Daydreaming to know myself,
Spirit, and God, I begin.
No more lamentation in my thoughts as
I perceive the golden doors are opening.
With the new situations, the surroundings
Frighten me; God whispers "keep

Going," as conscious contact whispers in me,
It grows, my courage grows.
Fear trying to dominate, but, faith and trust in
God becomes stronger to overcome.
I am engulfed with courage and strength
To face the challenges;
With determination and faith, God has
Straighten my path.
With the perception of the world,
A new creature is born with rejuvenation.
To excel in every angle,
I now exercise the strength within me.
Now with opportunity available in abundance,
So friendly becomes the world.
Moving with excitement, experiencing the
Miracle of faith I now possess.
God is available with us always.
Seek and receive him.

FAITH

<u>AFFILIATED QUOTE:</u>

"Faith is to believe with confidence that things we cannot see
and hope for with assurance will actually happen.
By faith, we are submissive to God. By faith, we are obedient to
God. By faith, we put God in the driver's seat for guidance; so
we leave things in God's control. Therefore, we must look at our
behavior and direct it in a horizontal and parallel path with
God's purpose".

Faith

The burning and earnest expectation
Of things, transform my faith.
In faith, more than I can realize
God is doing for his people.
In the darkened hours of
Despair that overcomes me,
Forget not I do of the strength that
Comfort me. Preoccupy with problems,
I seek an attitude of expectancy;
Combating this spiritual gap,
Faith in God is needed for victory.
I pray for acceptance to guide me toward faith.
Assurance, anticipation, and
Confidence based on past experience.
Faith within me fails; hope declines;
Depression dominates.
My spirits teach me to continue
To steadfastness hold fast.
With the renewed spirit within,
Together I situate myself;
With a clear perspective of the world,
Ego boosted, eyes opened wider.
Untouchable I stay with immeasurable
Peace bestowed from above;
God is able immeasurably to do
More than we imagine.

My faith eliminates vulnerability through
Trust, belief, honesty, and openness; By faith,
I hold fast, hold brave,
Hold strong to reach the pinnacle;
Regardless of consequences, determination in
Faithfulness supersedes anything else.
Necessity of God's assistance to grow

Spiritually is significant; with faith,
I leave everything in God's control for
Rejuvenation and transformation for betterment;
Believe more deeply, face up to the light,
I hold. To a deep and strong rock
Obstacles, calamities transform my spirit.

Amid the tempest of turbulence,
I promised to stay faithful.
Though I stray away from achieving
The castle of my dreams,
The sweet aroma of success can
Be grasped from afar.
Hope is now dominant, and success seems smoother;
Healing process accelerated.
In a glance of the light, all seems to
Be collaborated. Thanks to my innermost
Helpers for being steadfast in my belief;
God is able immeasurably to do
Exceedingly what we ask.

IN THE MIDST OF CALAMITIES

AFFILIATED QUOTE:

"It's a stormy, rainy day; sounds of thunder and flashes of lightning saturate the atmosphere. Instability dominates as east, west, north, and south darken. None to identify; chaotic it stays.

In the Midst of Calamities

Uncertainty projected in life
Amidst existing calamities;
Darkness shadows the area as
The moonlight fades away;
Lamenting, screaming, weeping,
And moaning saturates the atmosphere.
Locked up in the Camp with weird and
Unpredictable souls;
Charisma vanished; depression overwhelmed;
Mentality exhibits vagueness;
Suddenly a man with a name,
Become a man with a number with no name.
As a period is engraved on my progress,
Life creeps to a standstill.
Preceding such, with the rosiest
And predictable hue, life existed.
I questioned Higher Power if this
Destination is ordained by Divine prophesy.
Conspired physical world entangled
The program designed for my operation;
The voice echoes, "I am with you;
Man has acted, by my might, it will be revised.
Suddenly, I realize it is not over, God is at work.
Life can be carefully reprogrammed
And worn as a garment of pride;
In the midst of calamities,
Life continues with the newfound perception.

The screen became clearer as
I scrambled amidst existing calamities.
Some stagnated; some gave up;
Some faltered, one step in upward
Sequence I advance, in the midst of calamities.
Fabricated charges portray evil
Character rendered as I was frozen;
Lucifer is at work. What choices are available?
Surrendered I did to the Lord.
The essentials of endurance and courage,
Absorbing, understanding, accepting, and obeying they are.
As a product of many, in the midst of calamities,

I reprogrammed myself.
In the atmosphere,
The energetic charisma penetrates through
As the glory of God is revealed as the sun,
Moon, stars reappear.
As I am going through the process of
Rejuvenation, energy and strength engulf me.
With the renewed spirit, rejuvenated I am.
Prepared for new challenges,
I put on the armor of God to direct me.
I now stand with the glory of God wrapped
Around I. Standing tall with head upright,
Solid as a rock I become;
In the midst of calamities, Set, I am;
Rejuvenated, I am; able to handle anything.

TRUSTING

AFFILIATED QUOTE:

"A way of life is to trust and let go; for trusting God the first time is our way out".

Trusting

In the blink of the eyes, disoriented
I am without the palm of God as attitude of
Trust, confidence, and belief fade away;
Chaos hit, perception changed;
I doubt the existence of a compassionate
God. I do not understand the situation whether
God may intervene unexpectedly.
Searching and focusing on the human predicament
For solutions in the secular world, I found none.
Coincidentally, I go through the
Word of God and mainly
Look to Paradise. Charisma of the Savior
I fight to keep it always within me.
I refrain from thinking that God is unable to
Work with potential problems such as mine;
I equate my circumstances to God's
Action in the past and adjust for victory.
The incidents of trials, tribulations, and triumphs
Of God noble men dominate me.
New situations, surroundings frighten me as
As long as they are prevented from paralyzing me,
I realize that it is normal to experience fears.
With trust, questioning God's ability to handle
Situation is deleted from my thoughts;
I cast my burden and character defect to the Lord.
Pointing fingers at someone else, I did not;
Unto myself, I did.
Dominancy God holds; control he possesses;
And the assurance of "keep going on" he renders.
Gradually, trust is rebuilt.
I take every opportunity to prove my reliability
Even in minor matters.
Individual effort is no more adequate,
As trust in God now dominates all;
No more fads, no more ideas of mankind;
Now, I know the secret to stability
Is obedience, humbleness, and trust in God.
With a spark of the light, rejuvenated
I am in the palms of God.
With new horizon, my attitude of trust,

Confidence and belief are restored.
Patience, obedience, and resources are slipping away.
I ask, is God nearby?
With discomforts in my life,
Over the inconveniences, I complain.
My inner-most helpers remind me to focus
On God's faithfulness; I comply.
Rather than fear and complaints, confidently,
I face a crisis.
With the newfound confidence,
I refuse to allow impatience and doubt to
Make me disobedient.
As I demonstrate trustworthiness and faith
In God, I seek privilege and freedom.
With this knowledge, for guidance,
I am encouraged to rely on God Almighty.
Trusting becomes a way of life as
I surrender control to God.
My faith increases as I commence utilizing the
Knowledge bestows upon me.
My dreams and beliefs, I now follow.
Selfish role, I cease to play.
I now see the good side of people I hated;
And the bad side of people I trusted.
Afresh and alive I am; new ideas and attitudes
I am now open to;
Recognizing the insufficiency of my efforts,
I believe in God to do the work for me.
To solve potential problems,
I cease doubting the ability of God.
Once again, I am a new creature sanctified
And ordained with new perceptions;
Without Divine intervention, now,
I know that I would not have made it.

BELIEVING

AFFILIATED QUOTE:

"Deep in my heart I do believe as is true for most; thoughts of thy own, truth as in within, as in thy private heart, in all that is within; I shall overcome with God on my side".

Believing

Oh multiple believers,
What and who thou believeth upon?
Belief you grasp.
Do not hold steadfast only to that belief.
As you believe,
Is it incorporated in partnership with faith?
Believing, integral part of mankind
Eliminates doubt and generates success.
Believing, sets doubt aside and increases
Hope as the journey becomes smoother.
Choose thy belief pattern.
Dedicate your life to the right path.
Choose thy best belief. God's way it is.
The Almighty God is the right choice;
His name, you proclaim.
Does your action coincide with his ways?

Not your action;
What sets you right with God is your belief in him.
Firmly grasp thy conviction of God. The truth, accept.
Holding on to thy opinion within thee,
As you hold on to the opinion within thee,
Steadfastness in thy belief in God is generated.
Outwardly, you go around proclaiming the name of God.
Inwardly, in Wickedness, you thrive.
Why proclaim God while thy attitudes and actions,
God Denounces? Believe in God's word;
For a lifetime stays his pronouncement.
With attitude according to the word,
Grasping belief and faith generates actions
Decide to believe in God; decide to trust God,
Decide to follow God's ways,
Put him in control of your life.

Outward actions, church
Attendance, prayers, and good deeds you exercise.
Are you right with God?
Being baptized, born-again, proclaimed-sanctified,
Elders, preachers, committee members,
Regular members; most of you are

Empty baskets when your actions are executed;
With just one step out,
The Concealed mask with the true
Color is exposed, exhibiting the usual
Habits of Infidelity, pornography, hypocrisy,
Gossip, profanities, consuming drugs, and alcohol.
You fool, who do you think you are fooling?
Do you think you can hide from God?
No, you cannot hide from him;
He knows everything.

God's at your
Doorway watching, waiting, and stretching his hands
Unto you; confess. Change your ways.
Humble yourself.
Do what is right in the sight of God.
Perhaps going to church is a family tradition.
Or, you attend church to socialize or for business contacts.
To your values, add not the Lord.
Do what is right; believe;
Obey God's word.
Wretched soul and self-proclaimed righteous
Who can deliver you?
To God, you surrender in sincerity and humility.
Decide to believe in God;
Decide to amalgamate God's ways and yours;
Then, God's blessing will saturate you.

LIFE IN GENERAL

AFFILIATED QUOTE:

"Life, incurable disease, as it is a weary pilgrimage as sweet as those by hopeless fancy feigned. Full of care it is as no time to stare, not even to stand. What is this life? Less harsh to others, it teaches. This life is a memory but with no pain to the wise".

Life in General

Life is it a snapshot of what it is designed to be?
Of course, an ingredient to the soul it is;
It is a magnificent pattern and better than any other.
You are the designer,
You design and custom-made.
Wear it in whatever way you desire: robe, suit, or jewelry.
Oh, ignorant soul, life is a pattern you fashion yourself; it is yours.
Precious becomes that pattern as it holds the future.
Some may accept it, but it is there to stay.
Do you care about others' perception?
Do you care about the design of your fashion pattern?
Arise, evaluate the pattern;
Amend the crookedness.
Amend the areas where crookedness has been manifested.
Set the pattern on a horizontal path.
What are you doing?
I see you are eyeing those with an artificial lifestyle.
Oh, it is the rich, the famous celebrities and
Athletes' pattern of lifestyle you admire?
Who really is your model?
Re-establish yourself.
That pattern is a fantasy.
You are day-dreaming, it is unreal,
It is not feasible; temporal is that pattern and may fade away.
You stand there pacing around;
You are lost, wondering, and trying to
Decipher east from west and north from south.
What is the right direction?
Cool off; settle down; control that emotion;
Re-evaluate, redesign a realistic pattern.
Recognize your needs;
With the help of the innermost helpers,
Seek god's presence and practice what he teaches.
Now you know;
You will gradually design a pattern fit for its owner.

Life, in the materialistic world, is unique,
Out of fashion, and worth nothing. But,
More is it into life than just the lifespan;
Yes, the lifespan is, lesser it is to life.

As you question the ultimate cost of life,
Materials gradually fade and dissipate.
The pattern is now briefly an extreme temporal residence.
The pattern as designed is here today
And tomorrow, it may disappear.
God, the source and creator of pattern;
To him, there is no remote pattern.
God is not only an ingredient of a good pattern,
But he is the source of the pattern itself.
Work hard to put your pattern together to be aligned with God's path.
Your pattern will be pleasurable,
Your identity will be eternal,
Paradise will be Homeland
Worry not about your pattern;
Possessions on earth are temporal;
You can't exchange them for your soul.
On the pattern, you will become a pretender
And maybe tangled and overburdened.
Worldliness or power is worthless.
The greedy grasp that is centered on
Worldly possessions get rid of that.
The available choice is free will.
Free, you are to follow the right path.
Make the best choice.
People who are unfilled and complacent are easy
Target to stray to the wrong path;
Fill your pattern with God's "Word and Purpose".
Design your pattern in God's way and
Live an abundant and secured life.
By doing so, you will experience with appreciation,
Benefit of God's salvation.
Now you know; the pattern is fashioned for you,
Just for you; only you; and all about you.

HOPE: SPIRITUAL PERSPECTIVES

<u>AFFILIATED QUOTE:</u>

"Hope is placing trust in a Higher Power. Knowing is the hope that no matter what the circumstance is, the shadow of God is over us. Believing is the hope that our trust is in God. Knowing is the hope that when we are weak, God is there to boost us and strengthen us."

Hope: Spiritual Perspective

Hope talked about it vaguely.
Significant as it is, is it relevant?
Is it the main core of humanity?
Oh, precious hope you are thy trust, reliance, and
Desire accompanied by the expectation of fulfillment.
Surrounded by obstacles as darkness overshadowed,
Once more, disoriented I become.
Lost is the beauty of the world. Solution, where are you?
Afraid, yes afraid I am; confused, yes confused I am.
The problem, oh that problem surrounds in evaluation,
Faith is lost. I swivel, I lean, I prostrate searching.
The alarm is not distance away. For Assistance,
I sound the alarm. Not too far away is God. He waits
At the corner, his word, point of view, and purpose
I stretch and grab. On my side, I am well aware that
I do not have enough time.
Seeking the best solution, I try to believe.
I appear weak and feeble;
So I search for an energizer:
The problem solver, spiritual food it is.
I now realize when problems overshadow me; so-
Called trusted friends abandoned me; not just the
Solution, but the solution itself is God.
So I stretch and grab the alarm cord.
On a continuous basis, I sound
The alarm over and over again with prayers for God to
Accept me. The word of God flashes ahead of me;
The Scripture dominates my consciousness.
To the word of God, I turn.
My life is equated to the story of Job.
Encouraged, I am to know that the core ingredients
Of suffering are strength and faith. With the newfound
Knowledge, where hopelessness is present, faith in
God generates hope.
Believing better days are ahead,
During bad or hard times, hope is what I need.
Knowing no matter how scary it appears,
With God's help, Hope will be manifested.
Hope generates courage and endurance to make me
Go through difficult times. If I had known,
I would have consulted God first.

Hope, reachable it is now. Praying is now a daily activity.
I continue to pray no matter how bad things appear.
Despair and self-indulgence vanished.
As part of my agenda, I now act upon hope.
The story of hope I openly share freely.
Future hope, I gladly talk about.
As it manifests itself with favorable results,
I offer hope as a gift to others in a simple way.
As the miracle is manifested, my heart is penetrated
As a positive occurrence is generated, my heart is penetrated.
I view life with determination through hope.
Once again, I believe that activities
Of the world should go on.
Busy I am trying to improve my newfound
Consciousness; now my contribution in
The world is to make it more beautiful.
As I view the world closer and with God's
Expectation, hope fill my mind
And love fills my heart.
God is always there with me, but my negative
Perception prevents me from seeing what
God expects from me. However, I always
Feel his warm embrace.
As self-healing commenced,
Pours upon me with water and hyssop,
The shower of rejuvenation it is.
I am cleansed and as white as snow,
Free from negative energy, the right path
I can now see with clear vision.
A new creature I now become.
Self-esteem becomes strengthened and reactivated.
With the newfound confidence, God's ultimate
Purpose will be fulfilled as my faith
And hope is regenerated.
With the motivation and new spirit within,
I am situated.
Hope is now dominant. New pattern
Becomes Smoother. With courage and
Success, I smell the aroma of vitality.
In difficult times, I now know that trusting God,
Putting him in control is the answer.

UNDERSTANDING

AFFILIATED QUOTE:

"Look at the attributes of our Lord. How great do you think
he is? Gain an understanding of his attributes: He is holy,
compassionate, kind, majestic, omnipotent, omnipresent,
and omniscient. Be aware that his understanding is beyond
any human comprehension."

Understanding

"In your mother's womb I shaped, formed,
And inside out I knew you." Thus, sayeth the Lord.
Common acclamation today, people proclaim
Understanding God, while they
Refuse to abandon attitudes and actions
That God strictly denounced.
Why conceal your true color?
Hide not thyself from the omniscient God.
In the beginning, the reasons behind God's instruction,
I understood not. However, currently
I am aware of the infallibility of God's
Complete wisdom and judgment.
During childhood, the importance of my
Parents' instructions I do not understand.
As I get older, I gain a clear understanding
The ways my parents try to raise me.
By maturity, I also understand that the only
Way out is by God's word.
Knowing this, taking action in God's path,
I adopted.

Understanding by faith without seeing,
Produces the urge follow God.
I look for God, I do not see;
I tried to touch him, but he cannot be found;
I called out his name, but he didn't answer.
I cannot even look at him. So I exclaimed,
"God, where are you?
He whispered with a consoling voice,
"Keep on praying"; just pray I will hear your cry.
I will grant your heart's desires".
In my mind, a silent voice echoes
"Why should a faithful God who refines
Thy heart is unable to grant the understanding,
Grace and peace you seek? Absolutely not,
The capable and sufficient provider,
Almighty God is his name.
The understanding I gained that
Assurance and confidence are the products of
Trust in the Almighty God. Myself, I start to
Understand better, from the Almighty God,
I seek knowledge.

Unto God, the center of all understanding,
Assurance and confidence, I surrender.
Relationship generates understanding.
Knowing a person may generate understanding;
Through active communication,
Knowing is generated only by the meeting of the minds.
Interacting, arguing, or abiding together
For a period of time are also ways of understanding.
African Queen possesses the ability to
Decipher my gestures, moan, or even sounds.
To gain an understanding of her significant other, she
Pursue it. Without being exposed, you may
Not know the world. Without peeping through
The Scriptures, you may not know the concept of salvation.
How to gain the knowledge?
Only by seeking it is done.
Trying to gain understanding without seeking,
Insignificant will the accomplishment be.
What do I want? What is wrong with me?
How do I feel? What is next?

I sometimes feel that I do not understand myself.
So I turn to God who with no limit in his power of
Understanding, thoroughly the Majestic God
Know me than I can comprehend.
With the willingness to help his people,
God fully understands the limitations of mankind's ability.
With my diminutive ability and limited journey on earth,
In front of my race is the Almighty God.
With others, I set in the rear of the starting line.
For people's life in this world, I do not
Understand God's real reasons.
Never free I am to disobey God just because
I do not understand.
In trouble, I do not understand myself. But,
The Scriptures tell me just to
Believe, have faith, and trust in God.
With his knowledge of understanding,
God the knowledge King understands me perfectly.
So I first move to obey God, then discover the
Reasons embedded my attributes and attitudes.

MY QUEEN AND I FOREVER

<u>AFFILIATED QUOTE:</u>

"We live together. We face all life's calamities together: the ecstasy, the joy, the benefit, the chaos, and the sorrow. I am with her; she is with me, and we are with each other. Our love has disabled fear and forever stays the union."

REV JOHN

My Queen and I Forever

Your beauty I hold as a shield against my hopelessness.
When my heart is feeble, your sight with a smiling face
I remember.
The errors and wrongs which I imply, you make right.
The kindness, patience, and love you extend energize me
As I become closer to you.
Your love brings grace into my heart and conquers
Fear within.
Together, we have been through obstacles, disappointments
And failures;
Together, we have seen the ups and downs of life;
Together, we have shared each other's highs and lows;
Together, we have developed faith, hope, and trust;
Together, we have matured through commitment, compassion,
Trustworthiness,
Unselfishness
And caring.
Our hearts and love, all we give to each other.
African Queen sits and stays strong on my right hand
Even though to break us apart, others gossip hypocritically.
They complain and submit false information about
Your significant other;
I need no other as African Queen fulfills all my needs.
For because love is what matters most, it takes essential
Priority implanted in me and African Queen.
The best use of life, is love; the best expression of love,
Is time.
The best time to love,
Is now.
Sacrifice, respect, and submissiveness are the essence of our love;
More and more with increased affection, with each passing day
I crave for my Queen.

Your beauty I hold as a shield against my disappointments.
Your smile and mesmerizing voice I remember when my
Countenance deteriorates.

Coupled with endless virtue deep, true, and dependable
Is the existence of our love.

In the Garden of Eden, our love is simulated with plentiful to harvest;
Where, we are implanted.
We pick flashes of brave loveliness exhibiting the sweet
Smell of roses.
African Queen, my rose, my sweet aroma of encouragement,
Generates comfort with consoling spirit within me.
Call out, let me hear you; stretch out, so I can feel you.
Seeing forever is your symmetrical body; magnificent it is.
Together, we have the Lucifer sniffing around for any opportunity
Temptation,
Selfishness,
Arrogance
Anything that will break up the relationship;
Together, we have people with two stain glasses trying to
Demolish our relationship;
Together, we have people applauding us for good deeds;
Together, we have people looking up to us as their models;
Together, resilient to all obstacles as a rock, stays our partnership.
With God on our side, our partnership stays unique as one of a kind.
No sun,
No moon,
No stars,
No flames,
No adhesives,
No chemicals and no minerals have a strong bolt to
Hold or dissolve what we share.
My wife, I commend you for being so resilient and patient with me.
Forever, I engrave you with me and carry you in my heart.
More and more with each passing day, I am in love with my
Queen and enjoy the comfort of a trusted partner; as
I crave for my Queen

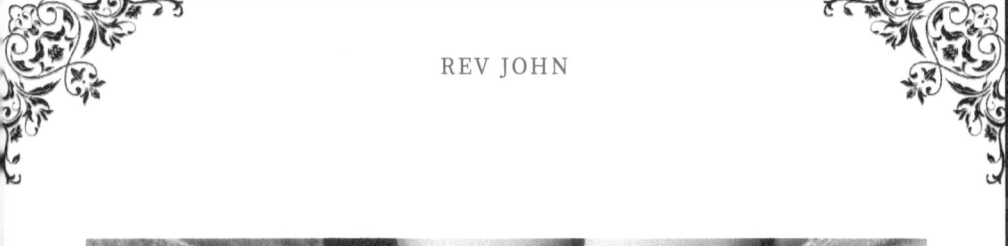

DEATH

AFFILIATED QUOTE:

"He was here, I saw him every day; I saw him a little while. His presence is felt; thrilled and lightened is his presence. Darkness attacked and engulfed; with grief all around, he is no more."

Death

Soothing and lovely death,
Come; your client waits for thee.
In tranquility you arrive without notice,
Whether or not ready.
Could mankind miss that mark?
Or plan for the surprise?
Death, do not be proud.
For monopolistic you are.
Though some vanished prematurely,
Mysterious, dreadful, and mighty most accept
And name thee. For you are not so;
For it is mankind's destiny and part of nature.
For mighty you are because those who
You think of, you overthrow.
Die not with sorrow, for existence
Continue in unknown dimension.

Die not in poverty, for no one knows, no one cares.
On the death of the rich and famous,
The whole nation recognizes and laments.
For with death, there is no rich; there is no poor;
There is no discrimination;
And there is no option.
Mandatory it is. In the eyes of death,
All is equal. So feel special not.
Why think about tomorrow?
Do you know the day or time when death knocks
On your sanctuary just to accompany you to eternal rest?
Relax people; it is an irreversible covenant;
Broken not, for it will be manifested one day.
One thing for sure, this dark moment
Every existing being will experience.
Who is your next client mighty death?

Is your mind made up yet?
In the day, death calls;
In the night, death calls;
In everywhere, death calls;
And in any place, death calls.

Is there a place deep enough to hide?
There is no exclusion.
Sooner or later darkness ensures eternal rest in peace;
And to dust or blazing flame you may return.
Grieve not for the deceased;
For remember only the good deeds,
The unfavorable deeds, remember not.
The will of nature,
No human or creature can escape.
In silence you lay fulfilling the covenant;
In darkness, you wait for God's final word.

Soothing and lovely death,
What's waiting for thee in the unknown world?
Some label you a villain,
But consoling is your restful visit.
Fit for an adventurous night in the wilderness,
A quiet life it is.
In tranquility without notice,
The world is of rise and fall pitches that arrive at will.
Beauteous death, jewel of the just,
You discriminate not;
Shining nowhere but, in the dark;
Six feet below, may be; submerge in water, may be.
When death arrived,
With mysteries it arrives that lie beyond human comprehension.
No matter how or when it occurs;
It crawls on you like a creeping creature.

Death, are you the ultimate end?
Do you avoid thinking about it?
Are you refusing to face it?
Are you reluctant to attend funerals?
Are you reluctant to visit the cemetery?
Is there a holding fortress that forbids death from arriving?
Think of morbidly, it is helpful. Think of death, it is helpful.
Reconcile with God; seek forgiveness before
The ultimate one rolls at your door.
To me, it will not be a surprise; to others it seems most strange
That they should fear.
Of all wonders heard, wonders experienced,
It is still a puzzle what death encompasses.

Aware that death is a necessary end will come when the fruit is ripe,
Encourages me to prepare and welcome it with open hands.
Weep, no more; groan, no more; wait for the call.

Worried? Sigh, no more; stress, no more;
With a GPS, it is coming.
Though death is handled in grief and sorrow,
The time is gone.
See you in the world of the unknown.
Goodbye everyone, my days are no more;
No more, I am; memories are no more;
Into darkness I shall vanish to rest in peace.
Unrecognized, abandoned stays
That name is imprinted on the tombstone;
Does anyone care?
Is someone keeping count?
Will anyone ever remember the day of departure?
To a new dimension I eye.
In silence, I lay consumed by nature;
To my Creator I return.

DON'T BE DISCOURAGED:
SPIRITUALIST POINT OF VIEW

<u>**AFFILIATED QUOTE:**</u>

"When you feel let down after a spiritual experience, remember that God's purpose for your life is still active. Continue in giving your best; never be petty; never be discouraged. There is no discouragement in a faithful believer of God. The storm may come; the weather may be severe; but you must stay constant in your endeavor."

Don't Be Discouraged: Spiritualist Point of View

Don't be discouraged; God Almighty,
You consult first; his attentive ears
He renders to us. Tell him what is going on,
How you really feel,
Submit your burden unto God. Then,
For additional guidance, with sincere
Colleagues or counselors, you
Interact with confidence and divine guidance.

Don't be discouraged nor destroy yourself;
Haters win not, unless hatred returned to them also.
Others may hate you; narrowly in their midst,
Mark not yourself. Discourage not,
Strength required; give your best
And stand determined.
Come weather, come wind; constant
You'll be stationary in this circumference.

Don't be discouraged or surprised
When for your faith, others reject
And persecute you; in steadfastness,
About your religion, faith, and Higher Power
Continuously tell them.
Trust God, for stubborn minds and
Harden hearts he will soften and open;
Deep within us, he knows us.

Don't be discouraged or worried
About the wicked or enemies
Who tried or trying to destroy you.
With God on your side, they
Will wither and fade away like spring flowers.
Trust in the Lord
With good deeds, he will
Give you your heart's desire.

Don't be discouraged; angry not,
Rage not, and lead not yourself into stress,
Nor lose hope. As temper is controlled,

Constant, you are with true valor.
Relentlessly you hold on to your vow
To be a pilgrim of victory;
Victoriously you finish in spite of
The tons of load you carry.

Don't be discouraged or give up,
People may try to discourage you
With negative comments or mockery
Statements in order for you to
Abandon your dream, but, continue
To follow your instinct and do what is right
And pleasing to God. God will reward
You abundantly according to his will.

WHEN YOU ARE IN A DISAGREEMENT:
SPIRITUALIST POINT OF VIEW

<u>**AFFILIATED QUOTE:**</u>

"You are wrong, I am right; does it matter who is right or wrong? Let us unite the meeting of the brains; then, in straight path we will march."

REV JOHN

When you are in a Disagreement (Spiritualist point of view)

When you are in a disagreement, have you ever
Stopped and re-evaluated the situation?
Think about it. Now, ask, is the argument relevant or
Based on a significant issue?
How amazing it gets in the midst of controversies
Arising from a conceivable subject?
In regard to such, upon difficult questions,
One should expect unanimity of opinion.
The solution to an argument or disagreement
Is listening humbly to what the other
Side is trying to relate. However, if the criticism
Is unfair and unjust, face the real issue as the
Critics should be perceived as feeling
Threatened or may be afraid.
Do not personalize your perception to such criticism.
Seek divine assistance.
To identify the real issue unto God you
Turns to grant you the ability to deal with it.
With a newfound vision, evaluation
You now perform the argument.

From east to west, north to south you move;
Shooting to the sky, dropping to the ground;
In multiple directions, all over the circle
You move around. In the middle
Of the circle, can we meet?
At first glance, it gets worse for a while;
Then, unified and better we become.

When you are in a disagreement,
Recklessly and foolishly becomes
The argument as the real issue is left untouched.
Attentiveness you exert from may be the culprit,
Jealousy or even envy. Selfishness or self-centeredness
Is the initiator of negative actions since you want to
Be like him or her, or the status, the position,
The appearance or even possession.
Without reasons, with absence of fault and
The implementation of things,

You choose to criticize and harass others
Rather than extending compliments.
Rather than facing the problem by dealing
And adjusting, Judas you become, sniffing around,
To justify the action, their envy and pride they adjust.
A shame it is. The reality, deal with it.
From the real issue, divert not.
As the clouds surround thee, take a deep
Breath, think and ask thee, is the argument worth it?
Is it over a significant issue?

Let the dogs and cats bark, growl, and fight;
For this is their nature. Let lions chase the
Gazelles, for God mad them so.
Let not your angry passion rise,
For we possess reasoning minds.
Let us live in peace and harmony,
To destroy one another, we are not made to.

When you are in a disagreement,
Central are certain issues to thy belief and faith;
Worth fighting for, is the religion.
Individually situated is the core of certain issues.
The differences,
You legislate for consensual agreement to be established.
Unity in essentials;
Liberty in non-essentials; love in everything.
The principles of the discussion they are.
Just as when Samuel disagreed with the Israelites'
Demand for a King; but, he assured them
That he would continue to pray for them.
Disagreement we might have with others;
But, praying and petitioning for them,
We must continue to do.
Our own disagreements with
Others must be settled before their
Behavior is judged.
With our behavior in the path of the Almighty God,
Our disagreement will be in peace and harmony.

Self-centered rather than love-centered
You have become.
The progress toward achieving essential goals,

You hamper.
Goodwill, trust, and peace are now damaged,
Generating chaos and anarchy all over,
Causing dents in a favorable human relationship.

When you are in a disagreement,
The consequence of your action,
You think not of; in neutral mode, you store.
Shifting through available resources, to the
Mountain peak, you accelerate, for a solution.
With appropriate subject matter,
In coordination, ideas you start generating.
Now you realize that differences of
Opinion need not cause division.
A source of learning, improvement, and
Enrichment of the relationship they are.
With mind in the right consciousness,
Dealing with the issue or discussion,
You now focus and meet the mind of the other.
The spring up attitude bring into light
Strive for harmony. Once again
About coordinated effort for solution,
There is allegiance to keep the argument on.
With persistence to neutralize any differences,
Common ground has found a place to abode.

Hurt you feel, love you express,
Disagreement you have, bleed you do;
Understanding and caring you need;
Argument brings understanding.
As with the human race, all are made the
Same with identical sensory; why not compromise
And seek equilibrium for parallel interaction?

HONESTY: SPIRITUALIST PERSPECTIVE
AFFILIATED QUOTE:

"Honesty is the backbone of wisdom. Honesty is truthfulness and self-respect. The initial action is to first admit the truth and tell others the truth. For the truth must be said and must be heard. When we do, we will recognize the good sides in people we hate and the bad sides in people who we assume are perfect. By being truthful, trustfulness and fidelity will flourish in the relationship."

Honesty: Spiritualist Perspectives

Honesty, the truth praised and
Starved with good fellowship, it is.
There will be troubles.
There will be wounds.
There will be pains.
Hidden wound, heal not;
But, just as honesty is to the heart and mind,
When exposed and treated, wounds heal faster.
In my lost times, I cheated;
I formulated lies; I lived in a sinful and deceitful way.
My relationship with African Queen
Became impossible as my concealed behaviors, she sensed.
With face down, eyes of my Queen terrified me.
Bringing corruption to my heart, in my track,
African Queen caught me.
I become a spoil and unfavorable light.
With no other alternative the truth, I revealed.
With the revelation, free I became and once more
I achieved trust.
With honesty within, I experienced healing and comfort just
Like lukewarm spring water.
I now stand on solid ground with confidence and
Hold my face upright;
It feels like a heated blanket on a blistering cold winter.

Honesty, with right and just deeds,
Delightful becomes Almighty God.
Like a time bomb ready to set off;
Double standards, lies, hypocrisy,
And dishonesty is the path,
Despising becomes the Almighty God.
As the sun, moon, and stars shine
Brilliantly in deeper tint through the dome;
Mankind recognizes how coordinated
God's plan is right,
Good and beyond human comprehension and imagination.
Humans are weighed down by the guilt of sin,
Becoming victims of circumstances;
Twisting the fact and trapped in deceit.

As I discover honesty is the right path,
I seek divine assistance.
All hidden rashes I reveal.
Free, I feel as I spill out everything and expose my true self.
I become rejuvenated with newfound character.
I now view African Queen as my dedicated,
Committed and trusted partner.
Now with confidence, I interact with
My Queen, and become honest to God,
As my path to salvation is God's path.

Honesty, the hurdle of life is the
Best policy for mankind.
When the truth is expressed,
In the long run, the result will be favorable.
Telling myself and others,
I listed distorted statements in categories.
Constructed lies become the path;
Truth and lies intermingled in a whirlwind.
My ability for discernment is surrounded by
Confusion and loss, it is.
I become alienated from God and my significant other.
With compassion, my innermost helpers intervene.
I surrender and allow them
To have the dominant voice:
"God is calling you" is proclaimed.
I confessed to God.
The move eliminates wrong and distorted statements.
Now in the right frame of mind,
I feel peace within and upbeat with my relationship with God.
With freedom within, in peace, with warm sensation
And cooling, my heart relaxes.
Now, an honest man I am without broadcloth
With open doors, I display my might.
Now I stay with a warm heart with closed zipper to my chin.

SPIRITUAL GROWTH

AFFILIATED QUOTE:

"God refines us through difficult and uncomfortable circumstances. We are being refined just as fire refines raw materials to extract precious minerals. After trials, tribulations, or calamities, believers' faith, character, and deeds become deepened, enhanced, and strengthened through practice and through overcoming life's storms."

Spiritual Growth

Savage fight among us,
Savage fight among others;
And even savage fight with Higher Power.
Spiritual growth, are you so?
Do you encompass the knowledge
That demonstrates survival?
Just a sight, may be.
So with your wagon,
To the stars you shoot seeking an answer.
In your endeavor, the clouds may block the view of the stars.
In the mind, you are aware they are still there.
If determined, through the beauty of the Gate of Paradise
You will pass.
On your way to spiritual awakening,
You travel through that beauty.
On earth, the key to opening the door to spiritual growth
Is adopting and practicing righteous ways.
Get ready.
Pack the accumulated possessions;
Hitch-hike a ride on that wagon, follow
Direction to the gateway of purity;
To a Life time of enjoyment, you'll ride.
The tree trunk,
The channel of strength from God
Will survive through severe weather conditions.
Branches serving God, you are.
Though wavering and blowing in the wind sometimes,
Steadfastly you stay; so is spiritual life to all.
As drought drives the root of trees deeper to find water;
Suffering, as essential core of spirituality is
Part of our training extending beyond superficial
Acceptance of the truth,
Generating dynamic quality of life
That Lead to the horizontal path of God Almighty.
To refine your life, allow Higher Power to take control of
Your vehicle. Faithful, you become;
Active, you become; compassionate,
You become; with others, share love;
With others, extend more love;
And fight to make the world a better place.
Now you view appropriate core of
Life is spiritual growth.

You study the Word of God.
You go through the Scriptures.
You become aware of God's interaction with faithful believers.
Now, are you aware that prayer, worship, and
Divine study is essential to spiritual growth?
Equipped you become with stamina and vigor
By actively engaged with religious studies.
Purpose you must have. Discipline you must have.
In winning the spiritual race,
To win the spiritual race, the purpose
And discipline is essential components.
Self-denial and hard work in spiritual life
Encompass grueling preparation.
There is a race to run. You must run the race.
Turn out not to the race just to run few yards daily;
Diligently you train;
Diligently you increase your effort and yardage more and more.
Be not a Grandstand observer of the Race;
A detrimental move it is. As you join the race;
A co-partner with God you become.
By training diligently and spiritually,
The pathway to spiritual progress you grasp.
Physical checkups you do;
Spiritual checkups you must do also.
As you sight the growing awareness of God's
Presence and power, your life becomes Rejuvenate.
Whether an impostor or a true believer,
Why not actively seek to grow closer to God?
As you game around,
Farther away you are situated from God.
Stop that foolishness.
With humble submission, change your ways.
Report past mistakes;
Learn from the lessons and thoughts recorded about God.
As branches are cut back to be fruitful;
Likewise, to strengthen characters and faith,
God discipline spiritual seekers.
As you endure the season of drought;
A growth pattern it is.
Now you are ready to
Embrace spiritual growth.

Look at you pacing around shaking off
The very emblem, the very life alert, the core
That makes you an overcomer.
Are you sure you know which direction you are heading?
To promote growth do you know that
Fruitful branch is cut back?
Likewise, do you cut back the negative attitudes?
Do you push back the action away from God?
It is a process.
For faith believers a process they should experience.
The end result is endorsed and stamped by God.
God uses His craftsmanship to refine faithful believers.
So as the fire refines raw materials
To extract precious minerals,
Likewise, going through uncomfortable
And difficult circumstance, God refines you.
New creature you become as your character
Is developed and enhanced.
Seekers of spiritual growth,
When spiritual disciplines are manifested,
Be disappointed not as life gets tough;
When the inevitable problems
Become painful and difficult;
Your composure, you keep;
Steadfastly faithful and dedicated, you stay.
With resilient stance during life's storms;
Your determination to overcome will
Be jump-started by God's booster cable.
To combat diseases and maintaining healthy lifestyle,
Physical fitness is used as preventive measures.
Likewise, spiritual health is used as
An essence in achieving spiritual growth;
Through practice and exercise of the
God's given abilities and gifts,
To sustain and emphasize spiritual growth,
Faith is nourished, improved, and enhanced.
A new creature is regenerated with good attitude
And better understanding of what it encompasses
To march in horizontal and parallel path with God.
Now with a renewed relationship with God,
Spiritual growth is achieved.

SUFFERING: SPIRITUALIST PERSPECTIVE

<u>AFFILIATED QUOTE:</u>

"Why are you so worried, confused, and feeble? As religious as
you are, you should be able to hold on. Go to the Word of God.
In my view, suffering is part of our developmental stages.
It is a tool and a teacher that, during the storm, it enhances
our endurance and perseverance. After the storm, it deepens
our character and increases our faith in God. So be of good
courage; claim your victory in God's name."

Suffering

Confused, worried; and not confused, worried;
What is it? To act or suffer?
Confused, worried; and not confused, worried;
Whether you act or not, suffering is still peeping.
Suffering oh suffering,
Unspeakable and deep;
Generating, rejuvenating, and regenerating.
The initiation of a new state of mind, you are.
Suffering oh suffering,
How intensive or how narrow are you?
Suffering oh suffering,
No one can determine or
Limit the magnitude of God's love for us.
God is love; we are his creation,
And inseparable we are.
Everything seems fine.
They are grabbing all they can get;
So are the "Fair-weather" believers. But, once adversity strikes,
As their superficial faith is destroyed;
Fair-weather believers are no more.
Put the roots of your faith down deep in God's ground and
Control so that you can withstand the storms you may face.
Understand we are of God's ways
By retaining hope while we suffer.
Only by experiencing suffering in full,
You will ascend with improved attributes.
A battle scar that demonstrates loyalty, so is suffering.
From steadfastness during rough times,
Perseverance, endurance, and encouragement are generated.
So converted into a learning tool, is the hard time.
Like a dream, when the cloud overshadows,
Raged and furious you become.
There is no forward, there is no backward;
Furious becomes the battle within.
With nowhere to go,
Submission to the Almighty God is the only solution.
With continued suffering, patiently you wait for God to act.
Depressed, disoriented; and not depressed, disoriented;
Symptom of failure they are?

Depressed, disoriented; not depressed, disoriented;
Maturity and completeness you seek.
Wrong assumption:
Good and innocent person never suffers.
Wrong assumption:
Those suffering are being punished for past sins.
Wrong assumption:
You are suffering because in God's eyes,
You are doing something wrong.
Like Job, our suffering may not be the result of our sins;
Careful you must be not to sin as a result of our suffering.
Whether temporary or enduring, real purpose of life
Is never destroyed by trials, calamities,
Tribulations, grieves, or troubles.
Despair you can be; impatient you can be;
Doubtful you can be.
When the suffering prolongs for extended period of time,
In submissive and honest manner, talk to God;
Petition him to work through the feelings and frustrations;
Then, patiently you wait.
Oh suffering,
You take our eyes off earthly comfort;
Oh suffering,
You expose fair-weather believers by weeding
Out the superficial ones;
Oh suffering,
You strengthen the faith of those who endure;
Oh suffering,
You allow our testimony to serve as an example
To others who may follow us.
Pretend not to be happy when faced with pain of suffering;
Endurance builds strength;
Strength builds confidence, confidence builds patience.
With patience, overcomer you become.
Now with God's acceptance and direction, comfortably you stay.

OPPORTUNITIES

<u>AFFILIATED QUOTE:</u>

"You should always be looking; it is flying all over; it comes in many colors; eyes it intensively to grab the right color.
Time is of the essence. For where there is opportunity, there is no great time. Distracted not too long, for while you stop to think, the opportunity may be missed. Be aggressive, do not linger, stay focused; as healing is a matter of time, so is opportunity."

Opportunities

Boom, baaaam, boom, baaaam;
Sound of the drum from afar.
I behold it may be; not awaken;
Dreaming, maybe not dreaming.
Just a breath away, in all direction,
The mass dominates the atmosphere.
I put on my striding shoes;
Accelerated I am toward the latitude.

A so-called trusted friend exclaimed:
"Fantasizing, it couldn't have been."
Hypocrisy, hypocrisy, oh thou Judas;
Who would not say so; at least, he tries.
Alert I am of the opportunity
Knocking on my back door;
Fear of what might happen,
I have not; full advantage will I utilize.

Incinerated I did of all the day's
Incidents at each night watch.
Rejuvenated and energized I am to
Continue the search at the glimpse of sunrise.
The most important opportunities may
Come when least Expected.
Ready I am by the might of God,
Not only by my might.

Though thousands may point their fingers on me,
Thousands to degrade me,
Thousands to discourage me,
Thousands to label me a failure;
With my integrity and divine help,
Engulfed I am with the ability, courage, and power
With perseverance and rejuvenated attitude,
The search for the hidden vessel continues.

Something showed up that might have been perfect,
But, negligence dominates.
Misjudgment from stress, financial burdens,

And tribulations distorted the decision.
To prove faithfulness to others,
Problems and limitations generate opportunities.
Derive from troubles are opportunities, as
God's power is demonstrated.

Overlooked, forgotten, pass by, ungratefulness;
Surprised I am not.
Staying closer to God I do,
When the bell is rung with a task,
The opportunity I wait for.
With no "shame face",
I extend lending hand to those who support me.
With the opportunity now within reach, I stretch out to grab it.

IN THE MIDST OF CHANGES

AFFILIATED QUOTE:

"Do not seek quick changes, for life moves like a turtle.
We learn about ourselves, make few changes; we learn more
about ourselves, make few more changes; we learn more and
more about ourselves, make more and more changes.
As long as we know about ourselves, we never stay the same as
we were before. In similar fashion, friends come and go;
relationship changes, circumstance changes, possession
changes and passes away; but, God, the Omnipotent,
Omnipresent, and Omniscient one never change; he sits high in
peoples' hearts."

In The Midst of Changes

Haven't you heard? It is reality; they are coming
Changes are coming. We must welcome them. Let us rejoice
And share with one another in bringing them to the atmosphere.
Is it needed?
Is it tougher than we thought?
Is it scary?
It is all about your perspectives and perceptions.
Maybe, it may feel good with excitement;
Or maybe, it may feel bad.
All that is known is that it cannot be stopped. It is recurring.
Manifested at all times, it happens.
Welcome to the world of reality.

Life is on a continuous path; it cannot be stopped.
Everything changes:
The world, family, friends, technology, sickness, medicine,
Age, and stamina.
New things are learned and done daily.
Better person we become with each step of learning and changing.
Afraid not of slowly growing;
Be concerned more of stagnated movement.
All grown up we are not with aging;
All done learning we are not with knowledge;
We are not with growing, we are not with learning.
With each sunrise, we wake up to a new world.

With mankind, making adjustment little or
Large is the molecular basis of heredity.
New conditions are generated,
That is customarily possible.
We learn and accept something new about ourselves daily.
No one who learns to know themselves
Remain just as they were before.
Turning to Higher Power to take charge of our life,
Station us to change a little at a time
And change a little, more and more at a time.
Life is its own journey as presupposes
Self-changes and movements.
Circumstances change, friends come and go;

In this fast-paced world nothing stays the same all the time.
Difficult it is to find any solid foundation
Not vulnerable to change.
Achievements changes, life changes;
Only hope in God should stay the same;
As everything else passed away;
But, only God is constant and permanent.
Detrimental it is to us with pretense of
Change in our attitude, beliefs, and desires.
However, changes parallel with God's path is needed as
They generate new purpose and hope.

All grown up; all done learning
With aging we are not, with continuous existence.
Changes must be made or else, like a fisherman
Without a net or hook we'll become. Old attitudes, you avoid.
Though something appears different, doesn't mean
It has changed. Every day we wake up to a world with new ideas.
We must change.
Just as leaves change with the seasons,
So be our opinions and ideas.
Look back at your experience during a difficult transition?
How was it? So in the midst of change,
Barriers are broken, and dynamic transformations are gained.

MY SIGNIFICANT OTHER

AFFILIATED QUOTE:

"My desire, affection, and attraction for you supersede anything else on earth. The affection I have for you arouses my delight and admiration with sparkling tenderness.
Babe, my love for you conquers all."

My Significant Other

My significant other, without thee, non-existence will I be.
With the beam from the sunrise, just the thought of you
Energize me. Peaceful I remain with the moonlight.
Significant you are to me as I share my existence with you.
Loving thoughts and fond wishes are embedded with you.
March with extreme joy throughout our union is the
Designated name: African Queen. United, you are with me.
Within my sleep, I behold your brown eyes glancing bright;
Radiating the atmosphere with a colorful display, exhibiting paradise
On earth. Within my sleep, I hear your striding steps, cooling my
Racing heart beats; so consoling and firm it becomes.

My significant other, I am so often at a loss to find
The words to tell you how greatly significant you are to me.
I compare you in my imagination like the stars, moon, and sun.
My African Queen, the most beautiful flower in the garden; you
Bring happiness deep within me at all joyous moments.
God has answered my special prayer for our amalgamation;
And God Know that my world needs no other but you.
My beautiful, my hunger for thee is powerful and strong;
Though tempted, with a weak fleshy consciousness, tilted I sway,
Shifting temporarily; but, immediately erected again to stand with thee.
My beautiful, I was tempted; but, long live my love for thee.

My significant other, those who stand forth against my love for
You are ignorant of true love. For my love as divinely sanctified and
Ordained, overpowers the gods as my wishes are granted by Higher Power.
My love is unconquerable; not even the pure immortal can escape it.
Lovers of beauty without extravagance, we are; lovers of
Wisdom without malign we are; with God's help, no matter what they
Do, solid as a rock we are to overcome obstacles.
True, honorable, and dear you are to me as a special
Mechanical device pays a visit to synergize my fatigued heart.
I will retain more joy than I can express as long as you never forget
How wonderful and beautiful you are to my eyes, heart, and might.

WALKING IN RIGHTEOUSNESS

<u>AFFILIATED QUOTE:</u>

"The question I ask is what do you consider righteousness?
To me, righteousness is perceived as follows:
1. Walking parallel and horizontal in God's path with
obedience and humility.
2. Not self-centered but self-less.
3. Dealing with others with respect and concern about their
welfare; especially, the needy, the poor, and the
disadvantaged.
4. Seek liberty and justice for all.
5. Not arrogant; not envy or jealous, and has no vainglory, and
submissive to God for courage, endurance, and
stand for what is right.
When we walk in righteousness, we enjoy peace within with
consoling spirit like a calm wave of the sea."

REV JOHN

Walking in Righteousness

Walking in righteousness, I proceed carefully with
The blessing bestows upon me from above. I utilize
Divine guidance as my GPS in seeking, exercising, and
Sharing honesty.
The clouds open, it rains; all things of old are washed away,
Generating a rejuvenated outlook of my life with hope and concern
About the welfare of God's creation and understanding of liberty
And justice. Respectfully I walk a straight line even though I proceed
With an Indirect path, but, distance from the ungodly and forbidden
Folks. Now within me, injustice I hate and justice I love.

Walking in righteousness, nothing scares me for I become
As bold as a lion; bold as a tiger; erected I am upright as a
Cobra. With a snapshot, I hold on to whatever I perceive and
Stand firmly.
All I do is look at fellows clamoring for what is wrong. The
Tyrants threatening countenance cannot shake me.
I transform with a firm resolve to waver not of the frenzy, a
Man who is tenacious of purpose in a rightful cause I become.
Now I am not infused into mankind from without, but, from within;
Into benevolence, righteousness, propriety, and knowledge I am glued.

Walking in righteousness, my ways, I change;
The right path, I follow;
Spiritual guidance I seek;
God's way, the right path I follow.
The garment of the Almighty God, I put on;
The garment of righteousness, custom-made made it is.
Once on, a new creature I become;
People now see me not for who I am but,
For the garment that covers me.
For people now perceive me as a child of God.

Walking in righteousness, I feel peace within as a river.
Within me are the consoling waves of the sea. As I become
As I become spiritually refined, to the commandments of God,
I humbly submit and surrender.

Righteousness and peace are twins, merge as one;
Inseparable they are just as man's straight path with tranquil habitation.
Better than wealth and riches, with a star-like appearance,
Rightful deed glows with delightfulness and integrity from God.
People flock around me; people adore me, and things become easier.
With the stars as the limit, shower I am with blessings from above.

DISCERNMENT

<u>AFFILIATED QUOTE:</u>

"Do you have an idea of what is right for you? Do you know what factors are negative to your progress? Have you evaluated yourself yet? Well, I tell you
It is time for you to get rid of those bad influences.
Associate yourself with people sharing the same belief, doctrines, and lifestyle."

Discernment

Justice I do not understand. I hate honesty and lead others to sin.
I cannot even distinguish between good from evil.
To me, materialism has become a central path of life.
Thinking only of worldliness and self-achievement become the path.
Instability creeps in and rules. My heart is broken;
My soul is despaired; and I become confused.
East, west, north, and south, where are you?
The cloud overshadows; it is pitched- black. An inch away
An inch away even cannot be seen.
What direction should I head to?
Help, I screamed. Help, Help, Help, I moaned; searching for help.
Is there someone to direct my cause?
Exclaimed a voice from afar: "Listen my son, relax, and calm down;
You are one of my chosen. I am with you.
Re-evaluate your priorities;
Readjust your lifestyle;
Discern your associates,
To register at a Theological Seminary, I am ordered.
Look no further, the answer is in front of you."
Hesitation was the initial reaction; then, caving in to humbly surrender,
I exercised. Aggressively I adopted new situations
And properly dressed and equipped myself for the new challenges.

The full armor of God I wear. Vigilantly, I stand firmly to
Undertake the challenge of the schemes of the unrighteous.
Like a scientist, I take off from the manifold observation of predecessors,
Who discerned and restated their lifestyles.
In fighting the disarray, as stepping stones leading toward
The straight path,
I select here and there in God's path.
With difficult circumstances all around, to grant me wisdom, knowledge,
And ability to enable me to make the right decisions, I called upon God.
I commenced training myself to fine-tune my conscience, senses,
Mind, might, and body to distinguish between good and evil.
The long-awaited rescuer appears in the atmosphere;
As the sunlight begins to penetrate, blanket of darkness
Begins to dissipate, exposing the illusive hidden mirrors.
With a clear vision,

I can now distinguish the difference between myself and the world.
Now with the ability to decipher what is wrong and what is right.
Realizing past lifestyle was a mess,
I abandoned all friends who are a bad influence.
The place I used to adore, I adore them no more;
The things I used to do, I do them no more.
Sanctified and rejuvenated, I am with arising discernment.

WISDOM DISCUSSED

<u>AFFILIATED QUOTE:</u>

"Wisdom is knowledge and an understanding heart to execute responsibility efficiently and to make the right decisions. Wisdom is a gift only from God.
It is more precious than gold and there is none to compare it to. So then, wisdom is the ability to discern what is best and the agility and strength to act upon knowledge. When you pray, ask God to grant you wisdom."

Wisdom Discussed

Wisdom, a growing process of constancy; appealing to you are the
Mind with everlasting satisfaction, operating beyond
Knowledge, and applying the knowledge in a life-changing way.
Ability to discern and judge what is best is needed. To act on
Knowledge, strength of the attribute is needed. Oh wisdom,
Where are you? Come, bestow yourself upon me.
Precious you are than gold; oh wisdom nothing
You desire can be compared to you. Plentiful is
The knowledge in the age of information, but
Wisdom, a basic attitude affecting every aspect of life,
Scarce you are, given, bestowed, found not. Oh
Wisdom, thou never come with a bounty of gold; for
The great price we intend, priceless and unavailable you are.

Wisdom of the head, wisdom of the heart, can the
Clouds be numbered? Can the prosperity of heaven
Be accounted for? Be thy endless humility; humility
By wisdom. Oh world, thou chosen not the better
Part, not realizing the closed eyes to be only wise;
But needed, mysterious to mankind, wisdom to
Believe thine heart wonders and afloat the atmosphere.
Oh wisdom, the masterwork of knowing how to grow old,
You solve the most difficult chapters in the great art of living.
With charity, patience, humility, and wisdom, there
Is no fear, no ignorance, no anger, no greed, no malice,
No anxiety, no doubt; peace and love overshadow.
Supinely stays thee and wisdom with a mission, finds a way.

Wisdom, decorated with accumulated philosophy, practical
It is, divine, it is, and God-like it is; God-given
Gift it is, resulting from thorough discernment of righteousness.
Strenuous is the pathway to wisdom. Searching sincerely
And persistently, there will be discovery during the path,
The true wisdom, compensation, and reward from God.
As seeds developed into trees, the trees bring forth fruits
The fruits developed from premature to mature;
So is the developmental process of God's wisdom;
Produced through a lifelong series of right choices made;
Moral pitfalls avoided; rejuvenated and renewed
From errors and recovery, all sealed with trusting and honoring God.
With the right choices made, wisdom becomes the norm for God's faithful.

RELATIONSHIP AS UNDERSTOOD

AFFILIATED QUOTE:

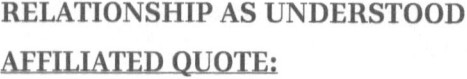

"Without relationship, there will be no universe. Everything works in cooperation and co-exists with each other: in friendship, marriage, partnership, profession, business, and government; all must have a healthy relationship to survive. In the Garden, lilies mature in unity, standing erect. Mankind should learn to live in unity with each other in all shapes and forms."

Relationship as Understood

Like lilies in the Valley maturing in unity and standing
Erected you are with compassionate attitude to all.
Logical you are, natural you are, emotionally committed
You are, realistic you are, and complying you are; from
The "lame", you abstain; with the "able", you comply; the
Straight path you walk leading to God's route.
Marching in unity in relationship is essential.
We receive, we give, and we get involved,
We make new friends, we extend "hands" to others, and
We interact in unity.
Like a band of wolves or wild dogs in search of necessity,
Successfully, they hunt as a team.
So lovely, friendly, and charming team player you become;
The relationship exists in a coordinated fashion.

The universe co-exists with each other in cooperation;
Each avoids crashing into the other. You fail to adopt peace
And harmony; so in darkness, you abode. Why are you
Looking extremely pathetic as chaos overwhelmed the atmosphere?
Now, headache, stress, and all kinds of ailments have engulfed you.
Your mere sight snapped up enmity.
You are confused.
You are beaten down. Now there is no more respect; no more trust
And no more credibility; all has vanished.
Take a deep breath. Evaluate the situation;
Eyes each other closely; unite the "meeting of the mind".
Now with respect, honesty, and humble submission, you interact.
With a rejuvenated attitude,
The essence of the relationship is re-established.

Fragile relationship is like friendship, partnership, and marriage.
A map of people who are strong, implying
And honoring existing rules,
Agreements, trust, and faith;
Backbone of the relationship they are.
To ensure that the full value is maintained,
It is as valuable as measuring grain in a basket.
Likewise, in relationship, compassion, graciousness,
And generosity, are reward in full measures.
In God's Book, physical and spiritual relationship
Are inseparable and pave the way for spiritual family;
The doors are opened,
The appropriate relationship with God is established.
Right attitude is born as the builder's cornerstone of all relationships.

CHANGE IN ESSENCE

AFFILIATED QUOTE:

"In the face of new conditions with humans, it is characteristic to make adjustments in a minute and continuous way until the targeted objective is reached"

Change in Essence

Life, the dome of several colored glasses, it is; immune
To changes, it is; like shadow tenant in 3-dimension,
It passes by, stained by darkness; created, regenerated,
And on earth's biological clock, substitute regeneration.
Life, the ever-moving wheel, cannot be stopped. The same age,
Do you stay forever? Let reality address it. The world changes,
And there are new things to do and learn always; and life still moves on.
By genetics we grow; but we must grow; and changes
We must make changes.
Change is like the ocean waves. Sometimes high, sometimes low.
Sometimes, we fall to the lowest status; we readjust, settle down,
Shake off the negative energies, and recoup.
We make new changes and make more and more changes.
Rejuvenated and erected upright, we stand.

Friends come and go, relationships change, circumstances change;
Possessions pass away.
Everything is susceptible to change, foundation even changes.
But, Higher Power sitting on his throne and never changes;
Monopolistically, he changes weakness, struggles,
And sufferings to virtue and worthiness from the inside out, as
He works on making major changes in attitudes, beliefs, and desires.
With these inner changes, faithful actions are born.
Refining and brandishing the best rejuvenated characters that is
Consistent with God's attributes.
Face the source of problems now; move not to escape from the problem;
For such action makes solving the issue isolated and difficult to realize.
To make the necessary changes, time changes and moves continually.
Continually, mankind should change according to circumstance.

LISTENING

AFFILIATED QUOTE:

"When people talk, step outside of your comfort zone; give your total attention to what is being said. By listening, you are uniting the meeting of the minds; thereby, letting them know that they matter."

Listening

The mind which plans them, the eyes which scan
Them, and the ears which are opened to them; carefully
And completely you listen as you achieve "meeting of
The minds", exposing the thought sought.
To a new way of life, open are the ears and eyes
Enabling wisdom to be heard and making us humble in
Giving and accepting advice, direction, and recommendations.
Convert yourself into the audience, feel what they
Feel what they feel, put yourself in their shoes,
And experience their ordeal;
Then, the thought from listening may easily be comprehended.

Quiet yourself, slow down, meditate, and wait for the quiet whisper.
Do you hear the whisper inside of you?
Listen again, now do you hear?
Find your chakras to connect with your inner-most helpers.
Do not talk; wait for them to initiate the communication.
Do you remember that the listening tool exposes the voice of the heart?
You must listen to yourself, listen to others, and listen to your
Innermost helpers as endowed by silence.
The truth and only the truth will the inner-most helpers expel.
Though rare for a person to hear what they despise;
Still, the benefit derived from listening overshadows anything else.

To the number of stars that cannot be identified, should listening
Be equated to. Similar it is to talking to a plant or tree; quiet stays
One party, only one voice is heard. Who is doing all the talking?
Have you ever stopped, think, and readjust your approach? now
Listen with undisruptive attention.
The other's point of view you now comprehend.
With the mutual respect, you can now enjoy
The notion of sharing ideas and expressing appreciation
For each other's opinion. The minds are now meeting. Ideas get
A little clear. You change a little, closer to an agreement you get.
With respectfully listening, you gain mutual understanding and feel good.

As whatever is in the heart, comes out of the mouth. With
Little changes made, closer to an agreement you get, and subjective
Parties feel good. Then, mutual understanding benefit is generated by
Respectfully listening. Whatever is expelled from thy mouth

Inwardly, comes from your heart. Commence cease and desist;
Then, commence again and then commence a little more; with
Acceleration, slow down; bring the atmosphere to equilibrium.
The grating roar of pebbles can be heard when listening; then
The waves draw back with slow retrieval.
We listen; we look sideways up, with no disturbances of
Heart, listening clearly produces the awaited visible outcome.

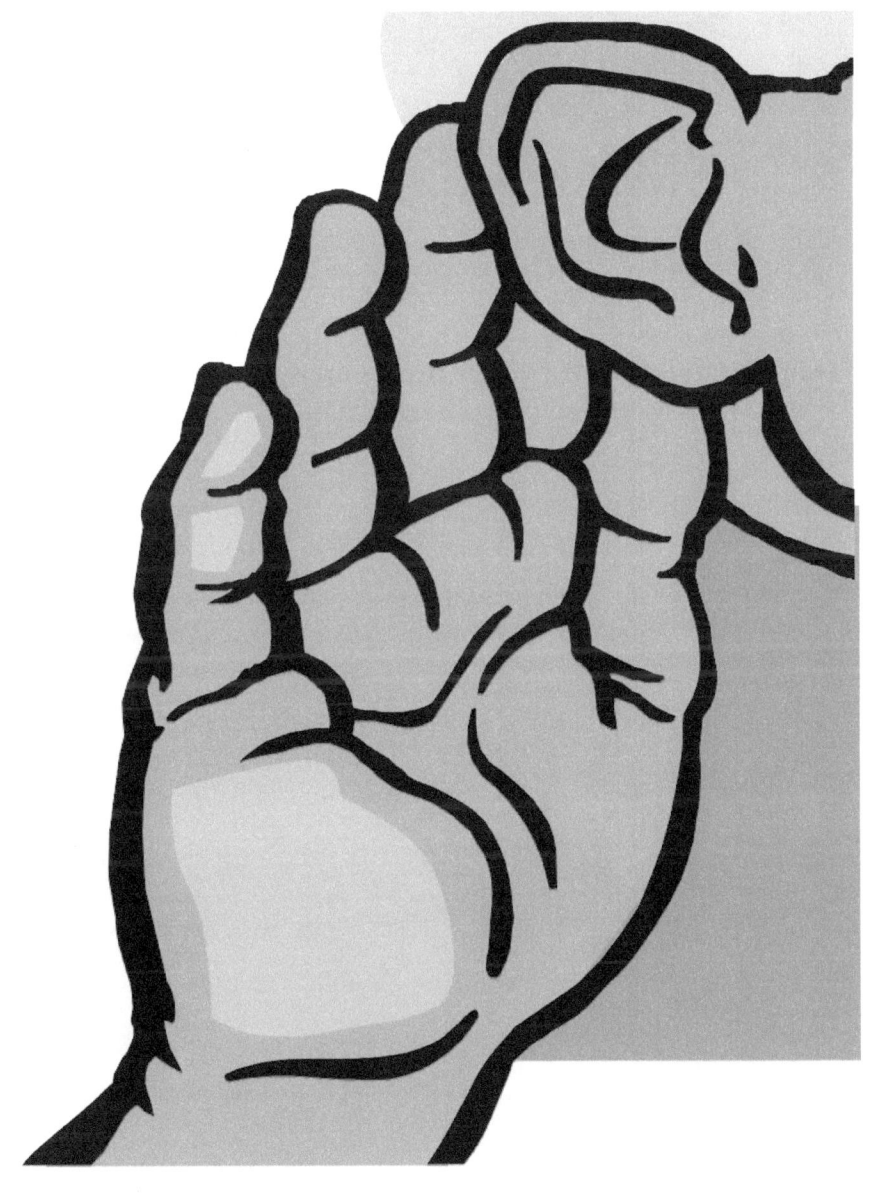

BE OF GOOD ATTITUDES
AFFILIATED QUOTE:

"When people talk, step outside of your comfort zone; give your total attention to what is being said. By listening, you are uniting the meeting of the minds; thereby, letting them know that they matter."

Be of Good Attitudes

Taunting all the time those we barely know.
Bullying is the right concept.
For we bully those perceive feeble.
Those barely unknown, dominion over them we establish.
Taunting them daily as thoughtless blow is executed.
Attitude of disrespectfulness is displayed, exhibiting
The consequences of many that are hurt. In the mirror
Of the mind, without any speech, the face project the
Secret of the heart as the eyes exhibit it.
The birds of chaos and sadness,
Prevent not from passing over your head;
But, from making nests in your hair,
Prevent them you will.
Hanging on to your feelings that make you
Feel bad is an excuse to exhibit unfavorable attitude within you.
The birds of sadness, quake-off you extend to them;
Birds of happiness, welcome you extend to them.
In the vigorous mind, by certain design,
In certain character, permanency is curiosity by certain design.
As the character of the mistress is sometimes
Inferred from the dress of her maids,
So equated are vigorous minds.

It is all about foolish pride, foolish it is;
We are injured through the culprit, embarrassment.
By senselessly occasionally lashing on blameless folks,
Such fallacy detours our progress.
Unnecessary move, it is;
Unnecessary gesture, it is.
Evaluate yourself.
What is bogging you?
Do you think it is normal?
No, it is not. You have a problem.
That Attitude is saturated with problems.
Evaluate It.
Now, visit the mirror again.
What do you see?
Now, with undesirable action, to hurt others,
Do not allow that false pride to force you.
Wipe off those negative energies.

Weave the warp and weave the woof;
Compassion, you include in your character,
Habit and manner within the attitude.
Now with corrective measures in sight,
Suitable readjustment is made to generate good attitudes.

Those who care about what their faces carry
And what design they exhibit,
Blessed they are with reasoning and rational minds.
Not because differences are projected
Indicating change has occurred.
With turtle steps, you open up with one step at a time,
And open up more and more.
The more you open up, the happier you become.
Around as good feeling is released within,
Your attitude will bounce around.
The more good feelings are released,
The more you feel better;
With the old gruesome attitude expelled,
You are no longer stuck with negative energies,
Occupying your mind with a destructive attitude;
Alive with love, joy, peace,
Laughter and full of compassion
You are encompassed with.
The old ways are washed away;
Spring up rejuvenated consciousness,
Now focus on productive issues.
With consciousness, you now seek the right attitudes.

A Samaritan is born, the helping hand you become.
In helping someone else generate happiness;
The deeds executed are positive and good;
With changed attitudes, cheering and directing
Someone else to be happy is common.
Happiness in someone else is now the best way to cheer you.
Similarly, it is to the relationship between roses and thorns;
Sorrow and gladness, pain and relief; so linked are they.
So it is true, you need no sadness, no pain;
All you seek is happiness and relief.
As resistant, feelings of goodness and badness
Like a river, it flows and over and over again, they keep on recurring.
Old negative attitudes, you must avoid.
They are destructive and possess a residual effect

That is portrayed within us
And interfere with our ways of thinking.
As you discern the right frame of mind,
A better lifestyle and a better person
Within and with others are generated.
As you are now aware of the falseness in your
Impression of external and worldly things,
Good character you adopt to generate good attitudes.

HYPOCRISY

AFFILIATED QUOTE:
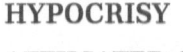

"Just like a chameleon that changes color according to the surrounding, the true color is hidden. You are operating with a mask. Your true self is concealed; the other is projecting a smiling face."

Hypocrisy

Pretending to be something you are not and having
No intention of being;
Oh what a hypocrite are you?
There are two faces existing in you.
Two faces with actions that are contradictory.
Visible, is one face;
Invisible, is the other face.
In which face you appear?
Are you portraying a different side of you?
You look so well relaxed.
Speaking lies in hypocrisy with your conscience
Sear with hot rods.
Jealous you are of my status;
Calling me mister, mister; answering me yes sir,
But, secretly in collusion
You are working to replace me.
What a shame.
How dear you?
Do you think your covert operation will be concealed and
Remain unexposed?
That heart of yours is full of worldliness.
Good intention is portrayed on the visible face, and in the invisible
Face, the hidden agenda are embedded.
Which is the positive one?
Which is the negative one?
Your primary intention is betrayal.
Under the table, lays your operation
Undetected until an unwanted and
Unfavorable incident occurred.
Like termites feeding on a wooden foundation of a building;
The exterior structure looks strong and solid
And the interior is all eaten up,
Deteriorate in a fragile condition.
Unexpectedly, without notice,
The entire structure collapses.
The actions appear good but,
Piercing is the motive, exposing
The good acts only for appearance's sake.
The action is missing a good motive and compassion.
Live your life in honesty;

Live as simply as crossing a bridge;
Live by making a decent living faithfully.
With no hypocrisy, good acts deserve good rewards.

Pretending to be holy,
You are not and have other worldly intentions;
Oh what a hypocrite are you?
In the today's world,
Existing are two categories of humans. I mean two categories.
Each with dominating overture: as a mirror and as a mask.
In which class you belong to?
Or with others, are you just tailing along?
How hypocritical can you be?
The public, you try to impress with religious
Knowledge and awareness by walking with
Your head upright, putting on fancy robe.
Now is your reputation the priority?
You neglect your character and on your reputation you focus.
Your virtues, you emphasize; others' sins, you expose.
Publicly you masked yourself with
Significant religious text while
Your heart floats with worldly possessions,
Recognitions and distance away from God you are.
To gain all the knowledge about
The scriptures, is not enough;
Professing to be a devout religious
Person is not enough.
Sincerity must be your attitudes.
The design of the inside should be projected on the outside.
Sanctified, faithful, born again, and a
New creature you proclaim to be.
All is just for a show; just to fool and Impress others.
Your words are just words.
How come you do not put them into practice?
Do you think people shall not notice?
You are like a fig tree that looks good from a distance, but,
Fruitless when examine closely.
Living religiously merely as a show
For purpose of impressing others,
Is like washing only the outside of a cup;
The inside is still dirty.
If you are clean on the inside,
Your cleanliness on the outside will sparkle

And not sham;
And it will be right in horizontal and parallel path with God.
With the absence of hypocrisy, labor, portion,
And care is rewarded.

Pretending to be a trusted friend while you are eating thee
Inside-out with your hidden agenda;
Oh what a hypocrite are you?
There are two kinds of people aboding in the universe today.
Two species they are with different stain glasses.
One stain glass is light and the other is dark.
Which stain glass is fit for you?
Look at you sniffing around, seeking a host.
You keep watch from east to west and north to south,
With unsuspected and vulnerable folks,
You hitchhike.
Every day you pretend as being concerned,
But your Agenda is concealed.
Daily you called, expressing empathy and concerns.
What are the calls for?
Are they to feed on new information?
Oh, I see.
Do you want to break up the relationship?
Wake up my dear,
The game you are playing will not last; it is over.
Rejuvenate yourself;
Change that undermining way.
Now the picture is clear:
You want to own the same house, the same car.
Retrieve from your closet your true color?
Show the intentions that are friendly and truthful?
Now, we see two hands.
Two kinds, I mean; one is helping hand;
The other is destructive hidden hand.
Circle the globe?
Wherever you land, explicitly it is stated the world's masses
Are divided and split into two stain glasses.
When their hearts are digging a hole for you to fall,
As chaos is generated on a recurring basis,
Friendly, they pretend to be.
The duration of such action is short-lived as
The mind grows sooner than expected.

Selfishness is like yeast, when mixed with flour,
To a different form it rises.
The real intention will be exposed.
As reality checks in, the realization of the existence
Of a two-hedged sword is non-progressive.
Positive attitude must be adopted to gain rejuvenation.
With no hypocrisy, the stained glass friend is now a trusted one.

SELFISHNESS, THE PERSPECTIVE OF A PASTOR

<u>AFFILIATED QUOTE:</u>

"I am the greatest. I am the only one to own it. I am the one that deserve it. It is my way or else. Selfishness, oh selfishness, who you are? You are arrogant to others and even to God. The destroyer you are, as your selfish ways ruin everything."

Selfishness, The Perspective of a Pastor

With arrogance and self-centeredness, your agenda
You execute. For your advantage only, it is okay;
Once it is an attempt to benefit others, a taboo it is.
Everything you try to achieve is at the expense of others;
With disregard, you execute your plan.
All the time, more wealth you need;
More possession you need;
Better status you seek;
More public recognition you seek.
All what you're doing is planting the seed of selfishness.
It is all about you and nobody else.
You are the best.
All the time you only fight to achieve the status quo and
Whatever will portray a separate and better you.
From deep inside,
The desires of your heart are darkened.
They encompass great evil and selfish acts.
In ruthless ways, you fulfill these selfish desires.
Your ambition, examine.
Are your ambitions only self-centered?
Or God centered?
Why don't you try the best ways?
God's approve path.
That path you seek and incorporate with your life.
With such path, actively genuine humility
And true perspective will be manifested;
And selfishness will be converted to dormancy.

All over the globe, using God's name for selfish
Gain, they dominate. In executing their strategies,
Fast and furiously they march into religious services
To feel better; to be accepted; to be one of the
"Joneses"; to relieve guilt; to form new relationships;
Or to create business relationship; Oh, what about the
Pulpit Pimps, the altar they use as their personal bank account.
Their true intention is hidden while gaining fame and wealth.
With mask on, their duties are presumably executed in God's
Ways as God's servants.
Their hearts, their desires are far away
Form that of God's.
Enough is enough.
Your true color, do not hide from the Lord.
Beware, repent.

The Creator for selfish gain, follow not.
Attentively, according to your deeds,
The Creator measures and evaluates you.
For selfish living, sent from above by
God are serious consequences.
Adopt the Golden Rules:
Love your neighbors as yourself;
Do unto others as you want them to do unto you.
With common courtesy and respect
You handle and execute others' interests.
With compassion and a selfless attitude,
Selfishness will become dormant.

Wise and knowledgeable people;
Distance to reach people;
How valuable or good are you to society?
In society, you are greatly needed.
With the excluded group, the selfishness of each person,
Spread like wind in its path, affecting multiple.
Just like an employee who steals from his company
Causing ruin to its productivity is selfish.
Or a driver who consumed alcohol
Before hopping on the expressway,
Making it unsafe, that's selfish;
A spouse who is involved in an adulterous affair causing
Destruction of the relationship and destroying
The family life, that's selfish.
Stop this immoral nonsense, otherwise the entire society will
Be contaminated.
The consequences are painful and devastating, and
By demanding your own way is also damaging also.
Live for God. Live as commanded by God.
Live for yourself, live for your family, and for
Others live with concerns.
Yourself, you readjust yourself; superficial lip-services, you eliminate;
Selfish desires and greed, you put aside.
You pray, you petition God to intervene and change you.
With the new adopted attitude, others
You commence treating as commanded by God.
The newfound lifestyle has made selfishness dormant.

TRUTH AS PERTAINING TO RELIGION

<u>**AFFILIATED QUOTE:**</u>

"Truth is the very existence of life; truth makes a relationship solid as a rock. When calamities strike and you drop to the bottom of the ladder, fair-weather friends distance themselves and flee. When you come out of your ordeal, those that still hang around are the true and trusted friends."

Truth as Pertaining to Religion

Truth, the trusted visitor of my heart; dominates
Like my significant other; within, it is as ruddy drops.
Extreme caution must be exercised when speaking;
Speaking the truth is like using a sharp knife;
It can produce good and effective use,
Or it can produce hurt to others.
Never handle a knife carelessly.
Likewise, with passion, truth must be expressed.
We live a righteous life through honesty.
By Being honest, we are speaking in a fair and
Truthful manner, expressing the way we think, the way
We feel, the way we perceive.
Statement remains the same with no need to remember
Anything that was said earlier;
For the truth has its own special knockout punches.
Winner is its name.
For the truth creeps in gradually and expose the hidden mystery.
Truth is what I seek.

Truth, in the story you keep straight
Like a line to make things a lot easier.
The truth, you keep simple.
The truth, you just say it. If you
Cannot tell the truth about yourself,
About others how can you expel the truth?
The worst thing is to lie to thee.
Darkness surrounds thee, uncertainty surrounds thee;
Just sniffing around, the true transforms
As lilies in the garden exposing
The bad side of people I thought is perfect;
And the good sides I see in people I hated.
The truth I seek, spring up straight vision;
The truth I seek, spring up rejuvenated plain heart;
The truth I seek, spring up better atmosphere;
The truth I seek, generate a rejuvenated countenance in me;
Part of my life truth has become.
Truth is what I seek.

Truth, always timely it is;
To yesterday, to today, to tomorrow it applies;

In multiple activities, in everywhere it applies.
Truth the ever-existing conqueror, always lingers.
Unagitated is the truth, everlasting
It is enthroned with oak and cedar strength,
Erected they stand resisting the fiercest storm.
Truth, from God, connected to God's characters, as changeless,
Rewarding and consoling.
To the truth of Higher Power, stand and hold fast.
Truth rested in closed doors when false
Teachings take front seat with greed,
Worldliness, vainglory, selfishness, arrogance,
All status of destruction; when these statuses are standard
And chained, behind a stained glass truth, is rested.
Thrown away are standards; thrown away are truth;
So moral of right and wrong become non-existence.
Truth is what I seek.

Truth, always with a clear picture with nothing to hide;
Truth with advantages, whatever works, whatever helps;
The moral behavior and justice it becomes.
Lies and false illustrations dominate the globe.
As truth overshadows the depiction of lies,
Uncomfortable the feeling becomes.
The ultimate source and direction, the word of God,
Withstand the best of time.
The enemy of truth,
Stubbornness blinds a person to the truth.
The culprit stubbornness you eliminate
To generate the best long run result of truth
And the abundant evidence of God's work in your life is exposed.
Accordingly, with the ability of mankind,
The truth of God's teaching is imperfect.
Obedience now is your key to get it straight;
For it sharpens and increases our comprehension and vision.
Truth is what I seek.

Truth, where are you?
Can you be grabbed by hand-stretch?
I sniff around to see if I can get a piece of you.
For my effort I seek compensation for me;
But, my effort failed.
To my knees I fall and for help,
I petition God to discover the truth.

Truth, the source of life,
The perfect standard;
The extraordinary phenomena;
Truth, the source of life is in
A class by itself, a star it is.
How wonderful are you?
Is everyone at liberty to choose you and live happier ever after?
If you always refrain and twist the truth,
How would you believe that someone else is telling the truth?
The streamline, God's path you follow.
Truth is what I seek.

Truth is decorated with perpetual smiling face;
Once engraved in it, nothing else to think about.
Wonderful, in all aspect you are with adoptive motive.
Waiting for someone to be adhered to you in truth,
Erected upright you sit.
How gracious you are?
Right action you are to adopt.
The master of the right thing you are.
Part of God you are; part of you God is;
Higher Power himself is the truth.
So mandatory it is by doctrine and tradition:
In truth we must deal.
A precious mineral we must conserve
It is the most valuable thing we have.
So flourish with truth within.
Use truth as the conqueror with domination.
Extend it to yourself, extend it to others;
Truth is what I seek.

Truth, the special light glows with clear vision.
As darkness surrounds thee, uncertainty surrounds thee,
Follow the truth for guidance you will receive as
It flows like milk and honey from above.
Look at you with your concealed self;
Why are you not expressing the truth?
Why are you not seeking the truth?
You accept anything, no matter what?
With that long struggle to express your true feeling;
You are lost, blinded become your view
Between you and the light of restoration,
The disorienting cloud it is, the cloud of chaos.

In your heart, in your thought,
Truthful will it be for you to believe?
What is true in you?
As it stands, difficult it is in accepting the truth;
Difficult it is than outrageous lies, to spot the truth.
Humble submission for God's guidance is the right path.

LIFESTYLE IN SPIRITUAL PERSPECTIVE
<u>**AFFILIATED QUOTE:**</u>

"The religiously inclined may expel a lifestyle foreign to the norm. They strive to be godlike by following God's path; by so doing, eliminating worldliness from their very existence. Models they are as they set a good example to others so that they may also learn from the lifestyle and maybe eventually, evaluate their own lifestyle. We should always live God's way according to his Word."

Lifestyle In Spiritual Perspective

On expedition I set out for; dashing down the mountains,
Leaping through the valleys I exert;
Walking through the green lands;
Playing in the creeks;
Flowing down the Stream and River; and
The rough Sea and treacherous Ocean, I flow through.
Sun bath I take; everywhere my eyes take me, I employ.
Trials, tribulations, and disappointments
Become part of life's journey,
Forcing different directions like gum sticks to a cloth.
Side tracking on detours that lead to failure,
I avoid. Failure is not an option.
Straight ahead, I fix my eyes on the established
Goals on God's path; a firewall is built,
Resisting worldliness and identifying
Attitude that is negative or positive.
With a lifestyle demonstrating
Obedience and faith in Higher Power,
I am differentiated from my neighbors.
God's Word now dictates my rejuvenated lifestyle

On expedition, I set out for within the spiritual
Pilgrimage, each stage of life builds upon the other as
Encompass with the phenomena of difficulty.
Weakly and feebly become my countenance;
The new life's challenges, I stretch out to meet.
Torn of load rests on my head flowing
Like a stream with pressure and temptation.
How difficult it is to resist the pressure of dealing with life
Challenges I discover.
Oh, Stream of Thought,
Oh, Stream of Consciousness,
Oh, Stream of Subjective Matter;
Unite you are within as life flows and chopped it appears.
Like birds, life is made up of
Flying and perching, through a succession of turns.
Acceptance it is;
Rejection it is;
The familiar core is now a type of choice.
As my head spins, I no longer seek everything;
On my desires, boundaries are now the firewalls.

On expedition I set out for with pain and tragedy in suffering;
I rejoice as my inner-most helpers remind me
That suffering is the route of character enhancement and strength.
Diligently, I trained with patience;
To be victorious despite hurdles and
Despite the hurdles and shuttles through the oceans,
Victory I am erected to proclaim.
I view life from a big screen;
With coordinated effort,
Mixture of elements interact from all corners,
Sniffing and eyeing the appropriate action.
My daily routine is coordinated with patience,
Time and determination, continuous practice,
Energy and vision;
With the vision of consciousness flowing through,
My spiritual path and character development
Improve horizontally with an enhanced perseverance and
Deepen trust in God;
With God, a closer relationship is established;
Endurance, courage, and ability to grow are now gradually visible.

On expedition, I set out for as the race begins;
Multiple others join the race seeking the right path;
To the race conductor, a list of needed items I submit.
From challenges to challenges,
From overcoming to overcoming,
From victories to victories, I move.
From undetermined origination,
There comes the guidance vehicle, the shining bright light,
Northern Star is the identification.
Viewing the wonderful stream of my consciousness,
I generate continuous changes to my brain as
Doubt within is melted away;
A new look is created in my life.
Words are no longer just words;
My words are corroborated by my actions.
When others take, I give;
When others hate, I love and help;
When others are abused, I comfort.
With such a humble, submissive attitude,
Established is my rejuvenated lifestyle.

REV JOHN

On expedition, I set out for with vigor and stamina, the
Race as my core journey is commenced to achieve Godly reward;
I diligently train with dependency on my spiritual progress.
Responsible I am for my own spiritual condition by maximizing the use
Of what God has entrusted in me.
In the branches of chance, with facet
Choices, lifestyle exists.
The right one, the appropriate one,
With guidance and diligent action, I eye.
At first glance, it's cloudy;
Discernment seems impossible.
Corrupt with fame, status, recognition, strength,
Wealth, adultery, drunkenness, I am engulfed.
It is like pulling a heavy chain.
Thanks nature for interplaying positive
Identification within me for what God has entrusted in me.
At will, I turn and grind the flour of my choice and taste.
From the grandstand, I merely observed;
Artificial display is exhibited as
I only jug a couple of miles each morning.

On expedition I set out for with eyes moving all direction.
Worldliness and vainglory become the attributes.
Into confusion, I am led;
Into sinful lifestyle, I am led;
Into chaos, I am led.
My eyes popped-open as an embroiled insight
To some wondrous power, has struck me.
With the new found guidance,
Surveying the surging immensity of life,
Hand in hand with my trusted inner-most helpers, I march.
A mixture of elements I am blended with as
Concealed agenda, lust, selfishness surround;
Arrogance glued with unseen tears.
The past hitches its way to the present and the future.
With consciousness centered in God's path;
Responsively, I execute the waves of obedience to God's word.
The pinnacle above all desires,
God as my priorities is established.
With God on my side,
I now enjoy my rejuvenated lifestyle.

GROWTH

<u>AFFILIATED QUOTE:</u>

"One of the greatest arts of living is learning how to grow old, which is the masterwork of wisdom. Mankind's life is based on living in agreement with nature; as growth is the major or evidence of life. Incrementally, we learn and accept new things about the world, divinity, and ourselves daily. These life experiences change us on a gradual scale."

Growth

A progression from a simple form to a more complex
One; similarly, no one who learns to know himself
Remains just as they were before; so is growth.
No matter how tall your grandfather was, your own
Growing depends on you. Learning to accept something
New about yourself daily, you do; as on a turtle
Space, changes happen deep inside of you. Each adversity
You eye, you question; and a deposit is for greater benefit.
Confidence is a plane of slow growth in an aged sphere as
Plants blossom through the ground.
Just as growth generates
A little more wisdom, knowledge, and understanding of the world;
A little more secure, settled, and sensitive toward relationships;
A little more perception and reality of things unknown; and
A little more control of your own desire, anxiety, and destiny.
Though painful, problems and difficulties are character developers
As they generate source of opportunities for positive growth.
Trials and tribulations are like deep roots set into the soil of positive changes
The deeper they penetrate, the stronger they become.
Through the storms, high tides, and high winds we slide
Through with glimpse of light, generating strength that
Assist in the achievement of successful growth.

A progression from an insignificant form to an
Unexpected sophisticated form; just like it is
In our springtime, everyday has its hidden development
In the mind; as it has on earth when the new
Curly stems are getting ready to shoot off the
Ground and keep the rhythm in their dancing.
Exhibiting charisma; so is growth in humanity.
There is not only one world; there is not only one
Way; existing, are many. Growth we must achieve
With new step into a new world and learning new things,
As necessity, growth generates both
Positive and negative outcomes;
A little more prestige, status, and recognition in society;
A little more wealth and possessions of worldliness;
A little more confused with problems from all angles; and

A little more engulfed with selfishness, arrogance, and pride.
Tested we are by God to deepen our capacity in order to cleanse
Us from evil contamination and develop our characters.
Just as fire refines minerals to extract precious metals, so
Refined we are by God through difficult circumstances.
Beautiful, strong, and spiritual
We become with successful growth.

PRIDE

AFFILIATED QUOTE:

"Pride, from the blindness of the heart it comes. Nothing else matters but you. In your mind, you grant yourself beyond anyone else and assign the GREATEST to your name, only thinking highly of yourself. Taking credit for work done, while deep inside you are aware it is done by God's strength. Do not allow this deceptive element to drive you to sin."

Pride

Oh eloquent; successful, mighty, and just you seem;
With all ambition you have been drawn together and
With your strength you cover the entire hemisphere.
Oh selfish one; oh inconsiderate one; oh cruel one;
What planet are you from?
Brain readjustment you shoot for as the answer.
With sensitive and gentle sway,
You yield to a contaminated society.
Push now with modest pride and surrender submissively.
Look at that, with such foolish pride
You are eating yourself up.
For your own glass;
Your own musical instrument;
Your own chronicle is that priced possession.
For blindness of thy heart with disdainful spirit is
Through the pride prefixing destruction,
To a collapse it leads.
The pride of a Man is the endurance and might of God;
The pride of an Elephant is the secret wonders of God;
The pride of a Crocodile is the patience,
Calmness and agility of God;
The pride of a Sheep is the trusted believer of God.
With greed, arrogance, or selfishness as the motives,
Sometimes hurt caused to others is considered a blockage;
Sometimes strike out at the blameless just for fun; and
Sometimes lash out at someone who gets in the way,
Just for self-fulfillment.
With respect, compassion, and humbleness within,
There is no room for foolish pride.

Justifiable self-respect it is; elation over accomplishment it is;
Righteous execution of things it is; the mass and
The mass and majesty it is; I am who I am, nobody else but me.
My prowess, who can withstand it?
Who can overcome what I have planted?
On Planet Earth, there is no existing being.
Complex is all as equated to pride.
Pride oh pride, forward movement you look up to and everything
Backward you isolate and refrain from.
A man you are with a mission.

A man who stands by his deeds;
But, allowing interference with thy ability to reason;
So obsessed you are with getting rid of anyone considered a threat,
Just to save face and gain credibility.
The conflicts you generate create a Barrier among people.
With seduction, to appeal to an empty
Head you have erected an empty basket.
The pride of a Woman is the artistic design of God;
The pride of a Lion is the strength and wisdom of God;
The pride of a Peacock is the glory of God; and
The pride of a Ram is the spiritual offering of God.
With insecurity, discontent, or
Excessive ambition as the motive,
Sometimes unwanted arguments stem from minor incidents;
Sometimes others are labeled enemies
And a detriment is resurrected;
Sometimes others are blocked just to be crowned the greatest;
With God's presence, heads will be filled with wisdom
And any gap will be sealed from foolish pride.

MY SHINING ARMOR FROM ME TO YOU

AFFILIATED QUOTE:

"The feeling is special. It is a feeling within me for you. The way I perceive you: your presence, the beautiful smile, the well-contoured shape, and the consoling spirit brought with your presence. The memory glued to my mind with your absence.

My Shining Armor, From me to You

I hold her beauty as a shield against all calamities;
I breathe in the sweet aroma of my tulip as my
Heart faints, sending a soothing pleasure deep within.
My love for my Shining Armor, is the most significant existing
Function in my life. My love is so hot as mighty nigh
That is can even burst a boiler; within is hot, as for her love,
I thirst.
In the midst of the cloudiness surrounding her partner,
Shining Armor shed tears waiting to see her husband.
It appears to be a vision. Maybe not, it is fantasy;
Fantasizing about the ecstasy, in every engagement, romantically
Pleasurable it is. With a beautiful display of
Elegance, her eyes send out stars.
Into my heart, her facial smile brings
Joy, filled with a consoling spirit within me.
The contour of her dimension is so
Symmetrical that there is no other existing to compete.
My Shining Armor, my Precious Jewel; outstanding you
Remain as the most beautiful tulip in the universe.
I sense your every step with an enticing
Stride bringing forth the most exciting feeling within.
I stretch out to touch you just to feel you; but, a mass forms
A barricade. My Precious whispers: "babe, I am here,
I am with you. I am longing to manifest myself for our
Consummation; don't worry, soon, success is mine."
At the gaze of the rising sun, all I see
Is the beautiful smile of Shining Armor extending
Comfort to me. Babe, our love will never dissipate.

I hold my strength as jump-started with your love;
You love me, I love you. Inside of
Me, I feel you; inside of you, I am.
Never before has love felt this way.
Great is your love for me. Great is what you
Extend to me, the greatest you are, with vitality you saturate
My core.
Close to you, you situate me; allowing, drawing, and making
Me part of you and united we become inseparable.
In our love, there is no fear, for it conquers all;
And the love of God inside of us generates

Perfect love within that casts out fears.
Precious Jewel, your love for me is patient and kind.
My Shining Armor, with your love, you are not
Jealous or boastful; you are not proud or rude.
Precious Jewel, with your power, you honor and
Respect me. Your entire self you humble to me.
My compliance to your ways, your own ways you never
Demand; but, for the love within you, my ways you
Maintain to keep me on the path with God Almighty.
Precious Jewel, we will never lose faith and
Hopefulness will always exist in our love.
Shining Armor, with your love you do not keep
Record of my wrongs; calmly you set it right for me.
Our desires we have set aside so that we can
Love each other with no expectation of anything in
Return. Our love Shining Armor will endure through
Every circumstance and will last forever.

OBEDIENCE: IN A RELIGIOUS SENSE

<u>**AFFILIATED QUOTE:**</u>

"I consider obedience as the state of willingly carrying out the wishes of others. However, as a religious person, I take obedience as submission to God's purpose; following his commands, resisting temptation, actively serving and helping others, and witnessing for Him. Base on love, is my obedience to God. I am a child of God; so joyfully, I serve him."

Obedience: In a Religious Sense

To the left you move; to the right you move; for a
Differentiated move, all is done.
Who do you think you are?
Do you only execute what you think you should be doing?
My dear, it is with intuition that deeds are executed. What on
Earth are you thinking of?
What kinds of things do you do?
Prevalently, not what is expected of the rational mind.
The gift from Higher Power, the Scriptures,
You must follow.
With an appropriate move, matters of worldliness
You now denounce. Your priorities, you discern;
And with God, you are identified.
The initiation of obedience, a matter of submissiveness
And humility exhibits a stronger understanding and better
Attitude, sealed with acceptance. Charisma flows like a
River as you discover God's will and live according to
His purpose and Word; with a detour now established
From conflicting interests, obedience is manifested.

You see white you want it to be blue. Nothing is good for you.
Let me walk a mile daily." No, he said, around the track
You run twice daily. "There is nothing to gain from running."
"Well, a trophy is there to achieve". Uncomfortable as I am,
I took off my shoes and lie on the bed. A whisper flow
Through my head "disobedient coward you are;
Be submissive and honestly surrender".
Stretch out goes my hand;
He grabs me and adhere into my heart his heart.
With my heart, my soul, and my mind
I am saturated with the light
As I walk with Higher Power.
The effective and offensive weapon I grab;
Available only by knowing and obeying
God's word is the religious armor.
Always sharp it is as a sword, obedience strengthens to
Transform into right. Stronger and stronger to exist
Enough to always be known as the philosopher, it becomes.
With the adopted perspective, obedience is manifested.

Spying from below, the ladder to climb to get to
God, is eyed. With repeated tries, you failed and fell.
Unreachable and overwhelming, you portray the height of the
Ladder, you never even tried.
Peeping is the relief device:
God with extended arms in standby mode, waiting to lift
You up and take you above the ladder to his arena.
Not from struggle, not from necessity; but, out
Of love combine with the might of Higher Power; so spreading
Is the free-will choice to make whether to obey or not to obey;
A personal agenda, it is.
Empty nest becomes religious rituals and ceremonies as
Obedience from the heart is more important than sacrifice.
With a mask on, you go to church services, active in the
Committee, give abundantly to charities;
All is done to impress.
To God, based on love should be your deeds, not for popularity.
With faithfulness regardless of consequences,
Obedience is manifested.

As the Rule of Nature teaches how the honeybees
Work humbly together with coordinated effort and act
Of order to erect their kingdom, as the quality or
The state of willingness in carrying out the
Wishes of others, as religious ceremonies, rituals
Are performed with attitudes of love and sincerity
Without expectation, so bestowed is the system of
Compliance, as the mechanism for success; beware,
The desolate pestilence concealed itself within, to
Devour everything in its path.
Refusal, neglect, and darkness are their force of power, bane of virtue
And of truth they are; if left untouched,
The desolating pestilence they become,
Everything on their path, they are ready to pollute.
Willingly onto God, humble yourself
And wait not to see the "bottom line".
For the time is now, the time is here,
And the time has arrived;
Act as obedience is now the core of all religion.

HUMILITY

AFFILIATED QUOTE:

"Let us look at doing little things like cleaning up after a conference, sensitive to others' need, exhibiting respect, and common courtesy and be Christ-like."

Humility

Being with a realistic self-assessment and commitment to serve;
Being not self-degrading;
Being with the proper saturation of God's
Sanctification with respect and obedience to him;
Being without self-depreciation, but self-appreciation;
And being with rightful pride;
So be the qualities you expressed with selfless virtue.
To bow rather than break is profitable,
So only by existence it lingers; since all cannot be heroes,
Someone has to sit on the curb clapping as the parade goes by;
These things are commendable for reality check.
Lose not the sight of the final result of humility;
As self-sacrifice is executed,
Joyous banquet awaits you with the "Host of Paradise".
The rod is hot and untouchable as God chooses you for a specific purpose;
For calling you,
God patiently waits for you to participate
In the wedding feast of the lamb as you join him in the labor camp.
With patience and humility,
There exists neither anger nor vexation.
With the release of self-centered desires, we seek humility.

Taking advice, leading to honor, bringing honor and
Bringing wisdom;
All the roots of humility contrary to pride
That is the result of harmful act.
Virtue all preached, done practiced,
And yet everybody is content to hear;
For in religion, preaching, teaching, or other work of
Spirituality should generate contentment.
Just as the Initiator of Christianity,
Jesus, occupied the driver's seat in commencing his
Ministry as willingly John the Baptist stepped aside.
Lose not sight of the benefit of humility;
Interaction with one another becomes
Appropriate as one person seat by the curb
To applaud, the other, participate in the carnival.
In endless virtue with wisdom and peace, there is nothing so
Become of mankind as modest stillness in humility.
Important is the awareness of self-worth and healthy self-esteem;

As significant as humility,
To God, self-evaluation for success and achievement is identified.
With childlike attitude, sincerity with humbleness you will gain.

Being thankful you have a chance to watch
The carnival from the curb side;
Being in a quality or state of being humble in spirit;
Being with freedom from pride to pride,
Arrogance to arrogance;
And being with a calmness of spirit;
So be the qualities of making coffee for someone else in need;
Picking up the mess after a celebration;
Petty jobs they are, erecting a building block;
As the carnival goes by, you generate ways of
A "good spot on the curb", you find.
Degrading as perceived by some, but, "Christ-like" it is.
Doing so, exhibits respect and common courtesy.
To God you surrender for a rejuvenated attitude.
The doors you now open for others;
Hands of strangers you now shake;
Interact and intermingle with others you now do.
Resurrected is a new you as
You discover a dominant newfound perspective.
With openness, inner purity and mistakes' admittance;
Purge with accurate perspective and security, humility is now within.

ANGER

AFFILIATED QUOTE:

"It is such a powerful emotion; it exposes the animal in us. Temporal insanity it generated in us. A fire it is; the words of the tongue once expelled cannot be withdrawn. If you are angry, take a deep breath; slow down before you expel the words. Words spoken in anger can be your worst nightmare."

Anger

The calmness of the waves and the consoling feeling of
The atmosphere sends a marching sensation through; then,
Unexpectedly, some noise starts creeping in.
In frenzy, the noise increases;
Chaotic the surrounding has become
With sudden roars and flashes of thunder and lightning
Generate unexpected sounds in distress and tumult.
In a whirling manner, the atmosphere is saturated with
Condition of warlike overture.
Through the starless air, lamentations and loud wailings resounded.
Words of pain, followed with loud and unruly voices
That is full of horrible and obscene languages.
Nothing can be identified, chaos filled the atmosphere as
The tongue is blistered with hateful, unpleasant, and
Destructive words.
The short madness is generated by a strong feeling of hostility
And displeasure;
As manufactured by uncontrolled anger, barbaric barking it is.
If not controlled, annoyance in the
Heart transformed to a "raging swine", ready to launch
At others.
The raging bull it is,
That contaminates minds and causes hurt to others;
The unspiritual thought it is,
That generates worldly concerns and desires;
Disorder it is,
That leads to dangerous emotion and regrettable action;
Evil it is, that brings selfishness and mistreatment to others.
With injustice and sin, anger may be justified;
But angry feelings must abide in a bunker for safekeeping.
With the right attitude, anger can be controlled.

In hell is seated the source of the tongue's wickedness;
Quickly idle and hateful words spread destruction with
Uncontrollable consequences like a raging fire.
A perfect candidate in standby mode scattered from
The uncontrolled tongue, ready it is to cause terrible
Damage. Words you expel, dare not be careless; for
Once out, neither can control nor reverse the damage can
Be done; for suffix apology is out of time.

Damage done, is the history;
Remain are the scars. As the sinews of
The soul, anger, possesses the soul, rendering a crippled
Mind for the feeble, overcome by its strength with a
Stuttering-riffle.
Barbaric barking of the tongue vents anger with outlandish orders
In a curt manner, that echoes in the darkness.
Anger, rage, and losing temper;
All birds of the same feathers;
Extreme destruction emotions they are.
The raging bull it is, that which destroys relationships;
Unspiritual thoughts it is, that violates God's command to love;
Disorder it is, that leads to bitter jealousy;
And evil it is,
That leads to mental stress and spiritual damage.
Like a thief,
Anger strikes and engulfs its victim with unexpected force;
So quickly it is poured out, but yet,
Vicious and powerful to be incurable and leave its mark.
On anger to eliminate bitterness, prejudice,
And selfishness, work hard.
Once implied with consideration in a constructive way,
Anger can be channeled.

JEALOUSY

<u>AFFILIATED QUOTE:</u>

"Jealousy, what a useless exercise you are.
You envy others with no reason.
God is the provider of everything; why don't you just ask
Higher Power? Jealousy is such a mighty warrior that it can set
apart the mightiest of nations and even the best of friends.
As a spiritualist, there should be no room for jealousy.
For the tool of receiving what we possess, turn to
God Almighty; he is that tool."

Jealousy

Oh thou mighty army,
The strong dividing force;
Ready to tear apart the closet of friends,
Even the mightiest of nations with thy possessed pride:
The blinding weapon.
Of force of a conniving spirit, you bring separation
To whatever victims you claim and even deprive
Them of what they are longing for in the first place.
How dear you are to be so good in concealing your true self?
You feed upon suspicion and move up into fury and then certainty.
The jaundice of the soul, you are;
The "weapon that slay itself" by its own arrow, you are;
The strongly rooted passion in the human heart, you are;
The tool of self-love, you are;
The demand for complete devotion, you are;
And the suspicion of a rival, you are.
Oh Jealousy, jealousy, the dangerous component of mankind's
Attitude, how can we eliminate thee?
You are smart; Connivance you are;
How can you be exposed?
Jealousy, thou create thy drama;
Thou generate hate, selfishness, and discontent.
Be content, be self-confident, then
Incapable will jealousy exists.

Oh, unimaginable envy,
The calumnious cancer that plagues
The body with your remarkable effect;
The overflowing pain with your conniving movement,
Soared you have out of the shadows of the night.
Accompanying you is the unrest you bring to mankind,
Contaminating everyone in your path with division,
Miscall, distortive ideas, and perceptions;
Instability trills thy countenance with delightfulness,
As you stain the world with an uncovered contagious
Disease, pouring forth thy unpremeditated strain
On the virtue of those two color-stain glasses of
Pleasing theme.
Void now of guile;
Void now of lust of gain;

Void now of pride;
Void now of avarice;
Void now of all existing sparks of jealousy,
The heart can be set on fire if not eradicated.
As cold-blooded becomes the heart with dominating wickedness,
Of the green-eyed monster that mocks the heart,
You must beware.
Be content with your possession;
Be selfless; imply love into your life;
And as a historic event, jealousy will not exist.

As a parasite, as a termite, jealousy,
You exist among thy host concealed and undetected.
As you fool the trusted heart, difficult is it to be recognized.
Are you aware of how contaminated you are with jealousy?
Do you know why?
Have you re-evaluated your lifestyle?
Now, for having it within, try to make sense of the reasons.
Dangerous it is;
For in manifestation as cultivated by your impart,
Is the blindness of feeling, the absence of compassion
Mixed with resentment of associates or rivals;
That is accompanied by ugly rage, generating harmful wishes,
Harm to others, all leading to sin.
Jealous rage, control; envy rage, curtail;
Set not thy desires on someone else's possessions;
Rivalry rage, control; unnecessary arguments, avoid;
For jealousy among the religious sect must be rational.
Do not be contaminated by this conniving spirit of destruction.
God's word, explore for a solution;
Love-centered, not self-centered, be an additional solution.
Seeking your attention,
The solution is saturated around you;
With precaution, to embrace the jewel, your hands,
You stressed out. Now fertilized with self-contentment and
Faith in a Higher Power, jealousy is now contained.

EXPECTATIONS

AFFILIATED QUOTE:

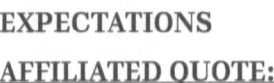

"Blessed is the man who expects from God through faith; for he shall march to the Promised Land by singing the songs of expectations. For as religiously as I am, I give thanks daily for unknown blessings already on the way."

Expectations

As I look up,
There appears a crystal blue sky with
The display of dazzling lights of multitude stars.
I commence searching for a shooting star of good fortune.
Maybe, one will display its beauty toward me.
Come shooting star, come;
Change my destiny.
Oh, there's one;
Look at that;
Magnificent; whaaaaaaaw...
A positive change in destiny is already perceived.
On the surface of the moon,
A smiling face of God flashes up as portrayed.
Looking forward to a positive overhaul in my life;
For centuries, I have longed for such a day.
With eagerness,
I await this least expected miracle.
With hope, expectation is alive;
For what is expected seldom occurs;
As to what is least expected, generally occurs.
So hope is what we should always implement.
Our mindset is of faith with the expectation that God will act.
Fears can be overcome when expectation is acted upon.
With sincerity in prayers,
Not by mankind's expectation, but, God will answer.

As I look up,
Throughout the days of instability,
Displeasure, stress, and sorrow encompass thee;
But, onward goes the marching band to the promised land,
The songs of courage and inspiration I sing.
Upward and forward, part of the active singers of expectations,
I move to be.
At last, with an accelerated move,
At this last moment, on hope,
I take a breath with imaginary relish so
Sweet that expectation whirls all over me,
Sending a consoling feeling of hope within;
I humbly surrender to God and for unknown blessings
Already in the atmosphere, I give thanks.

With God's help where it is least expected,
I set myself for his complete satisfaction.
In compliance, I move toward the essentials of his expectations:
Be obedient and trustworthy to him;
Live in a way of righteousness;
Comply with his commands;
With all my heart, soul, and might I serve God;
And finally, express love.
With newfound patience and confidence,
I set for the manifestation of the expectation of reality,
And I wait for divine deliverance.

PREPARATIONS

<u>**AFFILIATED QUOTE:**</u>

"God prepares. We are made in the image of God, so we must also prepare; for vital it is in everything that is intended to be done well. So it is a responsibility, not an option. For success to be gained, we must have a set direction that we follow; for preparing ahead of time, is time well spent; as planning can help alleviate worries."

Preparations

In readiness,
I embrace myself for the perceived battle.
Running high is my adrenaline,
As ready as it is to explode as a boiler within.
Visible is the effect as it cannot be ignored.
In desperation,
To seek the key to conquest in the world
Of the unexpected and of surprises,
I organize myself.
To fall, I will not allow myself.
For in the fall of an eagle,
Special it is; with providence it is.
If it is not now and if not yet,
But, it is nearby;
Around the corner it is and it will come.
In readiness for when it comes,
I set out to prepare myself in an orderly and collective manner,
As the unexpected outcomes are ready to be manifested,
My response I adjust to fit the consequences.
The condition of being made ready beforehand it is;
Extending to the plans made in readiness for some undertaking;
The secret whispers of others, I include.
For preparing for tomorrow, is time well spent.
For worrying about tomorrow, is time dumped in the trash.
Significantly, the choice is identified and differentiated.
For goals, steps, and schedules planning ahead are a must;
For God's guidance is a well-organized preparation.
Full of calmness, full of joy,
Full of liberty and freedom forward is the step.
Methodological is God; planning is God; preparation is God.
With systematic preparations, God-like attitude I adapt.

In readiness,
I can eye the world;
I can see the systematic design of Higher Power;
I can act as if tomorrow is non-existence;
I can consider nature as a careful special design of God.
I can establish a system similar to those categories
In mankind, that makes genuine differences.
In all that I can do, that will come, is preparation.

One that is systematic;
One in which the perceived outcome is addressed.
Responsibility it is, not an option;
For each battle sees the other's umber face,
As fire answers fire and arrow answers arrow.
With a well-done preparation,
Victorious is the result of alleviated worry.
In an instance, an overcomer I become;
With new perspectives, why worry about negative energy?
Why sit around procrastinating about what should be done?
Within my consciousness, such mentality crabs strong.
Unprogressive the ideas become;
The overflow of information is unbearable.
The best time to activate my retaining system is now.
So relaxation and meditation become the dominant factors.
Low I lay; nothing I do about the foreseen situation.
Awoke, I am by the spirit inside of me, with a consoling voice:
"Think before implementing action.
Long-range results may come;
But, only with careful preparation for today".
Just and responsible act I allowed on all subjective issues.
In all endeavors, as it is, when God is stamped first,
Well-prepared will you be for whatever lies ahead.

RESPONSIBILITY

<u>AFFILIATED QUOTE:</u>

"Responsible we are to spread out the word of God clearly and faithfully. For it is not only by words, but, by deeds. We must practice what we preach. For our messages and acts are nutritious food to the lost sheep".

Responsibility

Unpleasantly, it became as the situation crept around.
You can go to the top of the summit.
You can go to the bottom of the mountain;
You can sway all around;
You can stand within the valley and watch the mass go by;
And you can chant painfully.
All that is appropriate is grabbing responsibility, addressing
Negative issues, and sewing with cemented actions.
As we carry out a project, determination sinks in,
Courage sinks in; personal sacrifice sinks in regardless of obstacles;
As we carry out a course of action, multitude of incidents
Sink in whether as by position,
As by custom,
As by law,
As by religion.
As we carry out a plan,
Reality sinks in as the mission is generated, a dream is resurrected.

Unpleasant it becomes as a new way is sought to handle responsibility.
For as much breath you can take,
For as far as the eyes can see,
You act responsibly now with a plan, solidifying
The long range expected results.
Fair play it is to acknowledge your responsibility;
Others, you blame not for your faults and wrongs.
As the best way to live,
Being responsible for our own actions increases opportunity;
Increase opportunity increases responsibility;
Increase responsibility increases self-confidence;
Increase self-confidence increases from immaturity to maturity;
Increase maturity increases irresponsibility to responsibility.
With its facet qualities,
An alimentary canal with a big appetite is established.
The word of God is established in clarity and
With faithfulness, responsibility emerges as the core.

Unpleasantly it becomes as others want to act first.
Idly not you stand waiting for someone else to act;
Idly not you stand waiting for a miracle;

To the farm you go to toil in.
Multiple produce spread all over;
The right produce you must choose to continue smoothly.
Is cleansing required to choose the right produce?
What about born-again and sanctified? are they good enough?
Dare not,
Fear not,
Wiggle not,
Hesitant not; stretch out, it is all around you;
Search, study, evaluate, and discover it.
Grab what is right and execute the action.
With action, with acceptance of responsibilities,
Dwindle will wrong actions in your life be,
The core of all action will responsibility become.

Unpleasant it becomes as the surrounding atmosphere transforms.
Confused, you are as multiple colors surround you.
The time to deal with others is now.
Attitudes and principles sink in as you try to identify the colors;
Societal and religious laws sink in as your consciousness is engulfed;
Reality sinks in as you act justly with friends, strangers, and enemies.
Around you lay others;
Around you lay situations;
Around you lay uncertainty to existing situations.
With evaluation, the harmful situations,
Potentially and physically you move to correct.
To solidify the acceptance of responsibility to be clearly adhered,
Social and moral issues sink in.
Just like construction blocks, acceptance of responsibilities
Builds confidence and character;
With others, more and more respect you earn with time;
The complete project generates commitment and motivation.

Unpleasant it becomes seeking the right path to responsibility.
As avail to you,
Think first before you act;
For the effect of choices must be greatly considered.
The truth, oh the truth you teach it;
As you teach it,
Spring up becomes the acclaimed responsibility
Existing with the privilege of leadership as the truth is taught.

Just like sewing contaminated seeds,
Only bad fruits will greet you at the exit door.
Oh responsibility, the master of replenishment;
Oh responsibility, the core of the solution;
Attentively, you wait to be attached to a new agenda.
You are always sniffing around.
Can anyone live without thee?
Step up your reserve for foreseen responsibility.
The responsibility you now seriously adhere to.

WISDOM AS DEFINED

AFFILIATED QUOTE:

"Wisdom is knowledge and an understanding heart to execute responsibility efficiently and to make the right decisions. Wisdom is a gift from God. It is more precious than gold and there is none to compare it to. So then, wisdom is the ability to discern what is best and the agility and strength to act upon knowledge. When you pray, ask God to grant you wisdom".

Wisdom As Defined

Ongoing fight I hold unto;
Bleed I may, but, with all my strength I resist.
Perceiving it impossible to carry the Heavy burden;
Peep out of the window I decided to do.
With sight a little blurry,
Multitude of abstract figures appears.
In a flash of the light,
Transform they become,
A clear picture is portrayed exhibiting symmetrical figures
With multiple values:
As to possessing both the ability and strength of character;
As to act upon what is best;
As to living a life of simplicity,
Independence, magnanimity, and trust;
As to gaining to know-how to grow old with knowledge and
Understanding of the difficult chapter in the great art of living;
As to know the guide to life with the ability to eye life from
God's perspective and to know the best course of action;
As to know the basic attitude that affects every aspects of life;
As to have an understanding heart to execute
Responsibilities well and to make the right decisions;
As to studying the word of God and applying them to
Smooth and efficient practical knowledge;
So saturated is the DNA of Wisdom.
Ongoing process it is to become wise;
Life-long pursuit it is;
Part of life it is.
So be it; with knowledge gained,
Conjoint with practical execution,
Wisdom is exhibited.

How proud is the builder as thou elaborates the
Composition of the star-like building, though it is
About footsteps away along life's pathway, expressly
Stated it is to the demonstration of its composition.
Practical it is:
As to the tool by which trials and tribulations are
Overcome, generating encouragement and establishing
A way to enjoy living with good judgment;
As to allowing people to consider their steps and become

Enthusiastically seeking more knowledge;
As to make people respond to correction and benefit
From the corrections;
As to let people adopt the system of anger management;
As to divinity: beginning with the pursuit of trust and
Respect of God;
As to leading to humbly leaning with obedience to
God's purpose;
As to generating the ability to gain the differentiation of
Righteousness and disobedience;
It is Godlike:
As to be aggressively petitioning to be Godlike;
So saturated is the dynamic core of Wisdom.
With all the seeking and searching;
With all the knowledge and discernment;
With all the hidden riches and honor
Brought into light; proper attitude,
With the absence of arrogance,
As now sealed with rightful pride combined with
Obedience and humility, as
Wisdom is exhibited.

Look at the sky?
Eye its beauty; eye the birds as they zoom by.
I can see an eagle: the bird of the high and with
Prowess it patrols the sky.
View it as it passes by. Does it really know what is in the pit?
Is there a tour escort to ask? No, I guess not. It doesn't ask the mole;
But, with custom-made intuition, God made it so.
With mankind: as to in like manner,
God reveals his wisdom to those who fear him;
As to in like manner,
Wisdom commences as you get rid of
Foolishness and commence conquering fear;
As to in like manner, first-hand knowledge you gained from trial, errors,
And correction from observing and experiencing life's lesson;
As to in like manner,
Stagnated you abode in within the experience of wisdom;
As to in like manner,
Righteously, you live with prosperity as wisdom is utilized accordingly.
Otherwise, like putting your hands on barbed wire;
Only once it takes with no more recurrence.
So gloomed as categorized is the source of wisdom.

Beneficial it is, stronger it is as you grow;
The conqueror has to weaknesses.
The wicked path, you realize;
Head upright is projected, with eyes
On the sphere centered upon the wheels as it rolls on the right path.
Now, you utilize common sense in conjunction with good intention;
Expelling good advice, combined with God's approval;
And seal with a peaceful life, as
Wisdom is exhibited.

WEALTH

AFFILIATED QUOTE:

"Wealth, how do you perceive it? Is it the abundance of things that are objects of human desires? Of course, it is material objects with economic value. You seek power because you think wealth brings power. Well, note that with God, wealth, Power, and status mean nothing. What is in your heart, not your possessions, matters to God and endures forever. Wealth may bring about greed, dishonesty, or selfishness. Everyone needs wealth, but it is the love of money, instead of the love of God is evil to us. So do not dwell on wealth; as excess of it is the cause of covetousness".

Wealth

Flamboyant is the world of outward appearance;
A world of materialism, a world of multifaceted qualities,
Grabbing, snatching, a world, it is" regardless of consequences.
A way of life it is as of luxury, of good fortune, and of financial security.
The boast of fame; the splendor of power;
All that fancy images ever given; a priority it is.
A desire for plentiful it is to be combined with a special designation.
It is the desire for plenty to be combined into the name:
I care for riches; I care for possessions; I care for status;
I care for the quantity bestowed under my control;
I care primarily to obtain my heart's desires.
I behave, but, with a mask as I attended a banquet,
Where multitude others have the same intention.
Watching as something is being passed-around, all directions it goes.
As it comes to my direction, multiple hands stretched out to grab it.
Conniving, stretching out goes my hands, not to take a position;
Not to take a portion; but, to increase wealth,
I grab it all, build up a great fortune, and to increase luxury.
Motive for increase has become principal and necessary;
As with passion, a sort of societal likeness,
My love for wealth can be traced.
Taken up with the values of worldliness,
Wealth (the parent of luxury),
Spreads insensibility and as the sinews of affairs,
To my life, the core it is now.

All that matters is what I can derive from what I pursue.
I glance at only myself. Selfishness engulfs my consciousness.
As multiplying my possessions is a significant issue within.
Overflow, exorbitant living, Flashy lifestyle bring multiple friends.
As the earth is embedded with materialism, it is equated to paradise.
The earth is portrayed a little while as the spring
Bring a smile all around with extravagance, and then, no more.
The truth now flourishes within me, exposing melancholia.
A man with a heart is no more; for more and more possessions,
I try to sniff. The abundance of things is of my desires;
Just to stock up more and more useful and valuable goods.
To me, greed is good; greed is right;
Greed is the wonder machine; greed is the answer.

So piling on someone else burden, is easy as I move.
I eat up myself and become my own glass;
My own musical instrument;
My own chronicle; my own solution.
With such a selfish and arrogant lifestyle,
I eye destruction ahead, to my surprise,
A declining path suffixing a haughty spirit;
Creating an atmosphere as a sort of societal likeness,
Depicting the phenomena of greed;
Stressful and insomniac it is just thinking about decrease in possession.
Wealth, as so perceived to be the main ingredient of good lifestyle,
To my life, a detriment it is now.

The covetousness, selfishness, and arrogance dominate.
All around, instability flourishes.
In a confused state of mind, addressing the consumed lifestyle,
All over the globe I search for an amiable solution.
From childhood, the Time Machine took me back to grandpa's advice:
"Money is the source of all evil. If riches come,
Be graceful, obedient, and humble yourself to the creator."
Though high in status, high in title, renowned is the identification,
And proudly the household name have become;
As wealthy with overflow, with flashy and exorbitant living;
A wretch I am in need of godly values.
Otherwise, lost will I be and soon be gone into darkness.
Fondly do I wish; aggressively do I hope;
And fervently I pray for a miracle to extinguish such sinful
Lifestyle; an accelerated cleansing I sort.
Surrounded and covered I am with regenerated attitude.
With new perspectives, new attitudes, new devotion,
Unto God I humbly surrender for an overhaul of my lifestyle.
For God's promise of prosperity, I wait; a sort of divine likeness.
With a developed spiritual life, I found true wealth,
God's wealth with God's love as a mirror of concern;
Selfishness is now distance away and selfless glued into.
Helping the needy and poor is now my responsibility.
Walking in God's path,
To my life, it is now the main ingredient.

THROUGH THE STORM WITH AFRICAN QUEEN

<u>**AFFILIATED QUOTE:**</u>

"You went through the wave with me. When the storm hit, you were with me shoulder to shoulder. A rock fell on my head; you helped me to carry it and also helped me to my feet. Your strength engulfed me and implanted courage, endurance, and determination in me".

Through the Storm With African Queen

Pacing around, African Queen and I stand in the
Heavy rain storm in disorientated conniption as it
Suddenly pours down. Flashes of lightning and
Thunder all around; darkness overshadows. Our
Circle, once a peaceful and harmonic life is now chaotic.
The surrounding becomes a ghost town;
To rescue us, we find none. Multiple reasons cropped
Up as we seek solution to curtail the storm. Excuses,
Upon excuses, pile up. With no available rope to hang
On to, self- solution we explore and implement to
Stop the storm.
At our fingers' tip is the solution: To the Almighty God,
We humbly submit.
In spite of all the smearing of names, erected upright we stay;
In spite of all the disappointments, surviving we steadfastly hold;
In spite of all hypocrisies, solid as a rock our relationship remains;
In spite of all the trials and troubles, strength we find, not
Just to keep on going, but to go on victorious;
In spite of all the despair, healthy we are with God's might.
Being implanted with spiritual food,
Equipped we are as over comers standing firm in confidence;
Pushing forward in humility, on God's side we abode.

True is our love. Adorable fire; true love is in the
Mind ever-burning. Whether anyone else thinks too
Little or too much of this union, confused will
They remain with a partnership so heavenly coordinated.
In spite of all the trials and tribulations, unshaken we stay;
In spite of all, it doesn't matter how low we have been,
All that matters, we are still united in peace and harmony;
In spite of all, it doesn't matter how depressed we are,
All that matters, we have God's spirit to console us;
In spite of all, it doesn't matter being dragged backward through the knothole,
All that matters, the knothole is loosed;
In spite of all, it doesn't matter whether we suffered failures,
All that matters, we learn from the experiences to deepen
Attitudes and strengthen characters;
Despite all, it doesn't matter if we are stressed out that
We cannot even take one step backward or forward,

All that matters is with love, obedience, joy, strength, and peace,
Our innermost helpers and comforters counsel us.
With enough knowledge of our positive side;
With too little weakness for our negative side; smoothly
Smoothly together we harmoniously act to diminish selfishness,
Pride and arrogance; in God's path we march horizontally.

SALVATION

AFFILIATED QUOTE:

"For salvation is based on our attitudes, faith, and deeds directed on the right path with God's purpose. Merciful will he be to render us redemption from spiritual lostness to obedience and position us to receive his favor".

Salvation

Viewing the mountain from the valley, speculations fly all over;
Eyes are opened to the painful truth of grace as the multitude
Exist indulging in the illusions of hope;
So natural it is for a multitude existing with that sense of hope.
In contradiction, two colors of sounds of the
Songs of both sirens exist to be transformed by manifestation.
Willing are some to know the whole truth,
To prepare to handle what the worst is all about.
To know is to believe; to know is to desire; and to know is to act.
Not only solving the puzzle, acting generates the desired information.
With a staff of faith, a script of joy, a gown of glory;
Immortally, earned with a jar of God's acceptance,
Existing it is as nutritious food.
The deliverance of the soul from spiritual consequences
Of sins and the admittance to Paradise;
And the liberation from the phenomenal illusion of the unknown
World to eternal compensation of obedience to God Almighty;
So are the components of salvation.
Self-control and self-motivation we strive for by
Putting into practice our hearts' desires; in us, God is;
In God, we are; for his rejuvenating spirit to dwell in us.
With knowledge of eternal condemnation and eternal happiness,
The appropriate direction is God's path.

Gentle rain it is from Paradise as the quality of
Mercy pours down upon the globe beneath as the
Gentle rain pours with no strain. The shower of blessing,
Blesses those with ears, who have ears to hear;
And those with struggles, who struggle with faith in God as their guide;
And those with mind who have mind to learn about the truth,
Practice the truth within, as in their hearts' desires.
Establish for thyself a personal relationship with God.
It is not enough just to hear about spiritual stories;
But, part of the story we should become; for
For it is not only maturity in thy status with God by law, decree,
Or precept; but, maturity in sensation and watchfulness
In thyself to humble, obey, and trust in God Almighty.
The development from estrangement and spiritual
Isolation to a new and sanctified relationship in

Communion with God through the Holy Spirit;
The redemption from selfishness, disobedience,
Self-pride, avarice, and spiritual ignorance to
Spiritual fulfillment through the acceptance by God and
The direction by the Holy Spirit; so are the components of salvation.
Never again should the worldwide scope of salvation be ignored.
The appropriate lifestyle is living with God's guidance,
And God's purpose is embraced.

MY SHINING ARMOR AWAY AND AROUND

AFFILIATED QUOTE:

"When darkness falls, your beauty lights me up;
When weakness dominates, you neutralize my inner self and
boost me up;
When ecstasy is sought, you thrill me with your honeycomb.
Joyous forever stays our union".

My Shining Armor Away and Around

Feeble I am; unsatisfied, I am: unrelaxed,
Harmony I seek in my life for stability.
Darkness falls, twister surrounds, there is no way out
Searching for Shining Armor,
Pacing around is the only appropriate movement at that moment;
In a chaotic state of mind I am.
Confused I am searching for my implanted Armor.
A day without Shining Armor is a day spent out in space.
Busy as she is, Shining Armor busy taking care of business.
Now with dreams and admiration,
My Northern Star comes to me.
Shining Armor you are with a rejuvenating aura of my life.
A Princess you are to me;
A Precious Jewel you are to me;
A beautiful Tulip you are to me;
Babe, deep within me is my love for you.
Respect, I give to you; sincerity, I give to you;
Love, I give to you; trust, I lay down to you;
And ecstasy, we transmit within and through each other.
Seal is this relationship only by divine design.

Energized, I am; satisfied, I am; relaxed,
I am with the extraordinary vibration emitted by Shining Armor.
At night retirement, my Shining Armor glows all around.
At morning, alertness, my Shining Armor energizes me.
Oh my Princess my world, that voice at the speed of light,
With enticing vibrating sound, it travels within me.
Extended are my hands to touch her, but distance away she is;
Revere I did, but she did not respond.
All that matters, princess is somewhere lamenting her absence.
Rejuvenated is my attitude, charisma, mentality,
Confidence and security as Shining Armor submits to me.
Though underrated and perceived as feeble,
United I am with Princess as consummated from Paradise.
I love you, you love me; I love you more,
You love me more and more; and exciting and
Joyous will be our relationship as by God's love,
Our progenies will be precious and outstanding.
My Precious Jewel, my Shining Armor, my Princess;
You are mine forever, I am yours forever;
And sealed is the peace of God upon us forever.

COMMITMENT AS PERTAINING TO RELIGION

<u>**AFFILIATED QUOTE:**</u>

"Love you should have;
Patience you should have;
Compassion you should have;
Submissive you should be;
In all, to spice the soup,
You must be cooperative and obligated in all commitment".

Commitment as Pertaining to Religion

There is no love,
There is no patient,
There is no compassion;
As the hired man tends to the sheep,
With no commitment,
Only just for the compensation.
View across the bridge;
Look at that one,
Look how carefully and tenderly he tends and directs the sheep;
I am sure he owns those sheep;
As passionate he is,
As committed he is,
To the sheep he tends.
Out of love is his execution of duties.
Patience he is;
Compassion he is;
Essential as it is,
Commitment energizes faith.
Let us have faith;
Let us have commitment.
With faith, we dare;
We understand to the end; we excel.
With faith, we make right decision,
Right makes might;
Might makes achievement,
As understood, as we dare to execute commitment.
As tuned-up,
Refreshed become the mind and body as needed
In helping to shorten the distance to divinity by allowing a spiritual day,
Separating ourselves from our daily routine,
In renewing our commitment to Higher Power, generate concentration.
Religiously inclined we become to gain endurance
And strength in character with God perfect timing,
Our commitment, we solidify to him.
Toward the summit, life gets harder, commitment increases;
But, with obedience, humility, and genuine commitment,
Piloted are our thoughts, words, and deeds by God.
Voluntary it is by free-will;
Demanding and commitment it requires.
Selfless and understanding are the core;

Submissiveness it is to prevent chaos.
Not to surrender,
But, submissiveness it is I emphasize.
Not withdrawal, not apathy,
But submissiveness I emphasize.
To understand; but, as it is,
Co-inhabiting is commitment with obligation;
As surviving mutually with cooperation,
Combined with submission to God and others,
Willingly becomes the commitment;
Commitment it is to God;
For mightier he is;
The best he seeks for us;
Better care he patiently executes, superseding ours.
Commitment it is to God;
Our lives, our jobs, our possessions
Our families are entrusted to God.
To God, delighted we are in him to know him better;
To God, delighted we must with knowledge of his love.
In coordination with humility, trust, progress,
Achievement, and success commitment exist.
Now with the commitment, there's a mission;
Your intentions are being manifested;
There's responsibility.
The main objective is to deliver on the obligation;
So exposed become the supplies and tools
To unloose existing stumbling blocks;
With fear being incinerated not to comfort,
But, as you march through the waves and storms of God's path,
To commitment through suffering and hardship,
By the choice of God,
As steadfastly you hold on,
So genuine be the commitment as the shower of blessing
Blessing is poured from Paradise.

POWER

<u>AFFILIATED QUOTE:</u>

"Just as smoke and mirage disappear in a split of a second, so is worldly power. It is of temporary components that quickly vanish from the spiritually corrupt and immoral. But the power of God stays solid as a rock and eternally sealed with his strength and majesty".

Power

Renounce not the power of the omnipotent God,
For working from light to darkness and staying in darkness it is.
God is powerful;
God is true power.
For with faith in God, we desire not power.
For through salvation, God's power is bestowed upon us.
Desire not power;
For the desire of excess power causes mankind to sin and fall.
Power oh power,
You have infected the entire universe.
Within thyself,
Let harmony be of the power quietly made by instinct;
So as we see into the life of things,
Deep power of joy will be gained.
Worsen need it is,
As the powerful seeks increased power;
And weeping sterile tears it is, as the good seek power.
All with the wrong perceptions as it;
Distance to the Lord is added, leading us astray.
Thus, confused we are as destructive outcome is generated.

With God distance away, quickly vanish are glory,
Power and wealth from the spiritually corrupt and immoral;
As life becomes turmoil,
So uselessly becomes everything.
Everything now includes itself into power:
Power into appetite;
Power into will;
Power into universal prey.
With weakness and limitation, do not be despaired.
As your might be exhausted,
The alarm cord you pull; for God,
The strength builder will answer when the alarm sounds.
Admitting the futility of unaided human effort,
Combined with trusting God to save,
The secret of victory is displayed as God's
Power is exhibited with the acme of human limitations.
In the light, we rest with assurance that the power
Combined with love of God,
As God occupies the driver's seat,
Trials and tribulations we will steadfastly endure.

The horse, oh the horse as significant as it is,
Prefixed the Industrial
Revolution, in people's mind,
Dominant it was in the battle field.
The symbol of surging potency,
Projects the symbol of power and dominancy;
With action of man in show of power with authority;
The power of the visible, as temporary as it is,
Now dissipated and invisible it becomes;
But the power of the righteous unseen solid as a rock it stays.
Falter not is the power of God;
Diminish not is the power of God;
Chaotic not is the power of God.
For the power of God is everlasting.
His ability, strength, might, and sovereignty are eternal.
On human power, place not your confidence.
Though strong and stable it may seem,
Abused it is with no consideration for others;
Self-destructive it is with its own might;
Temporary it is and like vapor, disappears.
What will the action be with no power?

As in trust, accountable we are for deed executed.
As in effective means of influencing, compelling,
Or punishing others;
As in an ability to compel obedience or produce an effect;
And as in the right and control to command,
Decide, or judge; so is the core of power.
The absolute power; oh that power,
The mark of the beginning of spiritual experience;
That power, the Holy Spirit power;
The power of a new life,
The power of rejuvenation;
The only pure power, cleanses inwardly and outwardly;
Saving mankind through melting, molding,
Filling, and transforming the faithful to be godlike.
Godlike, the key for salvation;
Godlike, the essence for spiritual enhancement.
As monopolized is the Holy Spirit power,
Available it is only by faith, obedience, humility,
And trust in God.
Now we know that power through God is unconquerable.

GOODNESS

<u>**AFFILIATED QUOTE:**</u>

"Goodness comes from inside and expressed on the outside. We must do well the right way. When doing well we should lay aside the bad side and look at the good side of people. Dealing with a contaminated world as ours, good may be perceived as evil. So don't be surprised with such accusation. Follow God's example of goodness and trail his footsteps. Always remember, God works in everything for our good. He turns every circumstance around for our good".

Goodness

View the world, perceive it from all spheres.
According to your likeness, perceive it.
Falter will it be when you lean only toward
The so-called religiously and interesting group;
For with a mask, exhibiting
Exhibiting only what equates to peoples' expectations.
Two colors they possess: one hidden, one exposed.
Not enough it is doing well in a lifetime engulfed
With crucial mistakes of not following God's word fully;
Not enough it is to basically live good lives,
Yet failing to do what is most important;
Not enough it is that something is done well,
Yet cannot be implied as good;
For enough it is to measure all your deeds
By the Rule of God's word;
And to be the caretaker of their life, enough it is
Enough it is for true followers to put God on the driver's seat.
Even though persistence are our prayers,
God gives enough only to satisfy our needs,
Not what the petitions are. As learned we are about God,
He, the loving Father will grant what is good for
Us and steers the petitions in equilibrium.
Despair not; give up not, rest your hope; in God you always trust.
For out of seemingly hopeless situation he converts to good.

By the condition of bringing morally sound for us,
With the Rule of Right and Wrong as given by God,
Existing is the standard for everything:
Existing is greatness where there is truth, goodness, and
Simplicity; and beforehand nothing is so good as it seems
For doing what is right some of the time,
Content not is God.
Content will God be if the right things are done all the time.
Refrain we must from doing good the wrong way.
For in accomplishing set goals,
As important as the methods used,
So is the attainment of those set goals.
Do not complain, do not grumble,
Do not blame someone else,
Do not blame God when problems surround you.

For good it is to perceive the circumstance as an
Opportunity to derive good outcome out of bad situation.
To fulfill his purpose, not to make us happy but,
To make us content in everything, God works.
From complicated circumstances, God turns
God turns around into long-range good.
As taught from life's experiences with humility, hope,
And trust in God,
He will overrides evil intentions to generate good outcomes.

As evil deeds are confessed,
So commence a generation of good works.
Something inside of us is goodness;
Something not what we do is goodness;
For goodness, what we already are is just being what we are.
Try not hard to be good;
Learn, relax, and invite divinity to take control of your actions.
They are gone but, lives through;
For when good individual dies, perish not be their goodness.
The bad, oh the bad, a
All that was with them are buried as eternal darkness attacks.
The confession of evil deeds is the beginning of good deeds.
For in goodness there is value in itself;
About goodness, badness stays flaunt;
Generated by goodness, is individual's own merit.
Respect the positive side of another person,
For courage it takes to lay aside hate and hurt;
Look not at the bad side of people but,
At the good side you eye.
Ever existing is the truth or goodness realized by man;
For nothing that is worthy in the past, departs.
With faith, hope, and trust center on divinity;
With his ability, in all things for good,
God solve our problems.

SERVICE AS PERTAINING TO RELIGION
<u>**AFFILIATED QUOTE:**</u>

"With service, we are taught to care for ourselves and others.
We must look at what contribution we can make to life, not
what we can get from life. In the religious sector, service is the
demonstration of our devotion to God. We should serve God
with all our love, heart, mind, might, and soul.
We should serve him with a humble and obedient spirit.
We should always extend a servant's spirit to everyone.
When we do, we will see that we need others and others need
us. It becomes a lesson about the give and take of human
relationships".

Service as Pertaining to Religion

Service, the essence of humanity it is;
From God and others it is;
As with God there is no first; there is no last;
For we are best, we are worst,
And all service ranks the same to him.
Our hearts, love, and obedience he deserves.
A servant's spirit it is and extended it is to everyone.
House of Prayer, the way it should be;
Every member effort is essential for effective
Execution of functions of the same body, of the same God;
With the unique combination of talents;
The talents used for greatness; greatness comes from serving God.
Together in unity you work; in separation,
Divided and inefficient we will be; falling is the route of separation.
The message we must carry, not by words but, by deeds;
But, guided by love, part of the fellowship, should the action be based;
Spreading the rest of our lives to service is the idea;
As we realized and recognized the need of the world,
The tool is within us to offer,
Significant part of the world, we become.

Service, a good teacher it is;
It teaches us to care for ourselves,
Care for others is the main objective;
It teaches us, how valuable and worthwhile we are;
It teaches us, good feeling we attain from good deeds;
It teaches us, we will end up with more,
When with love, we give away;
It teaches us, that when we help others,
We need them and they need us;
It teaches us, about the give and take of human relationship.
Make two ears of corn grow upon a spot of ground;
Only one grew before;
Beyond all recompense is such service;
So be the essential service to mankind.
True service is service from the humblest person while it last.
Shining with bright aura, scorn not one;
Protect the lingering dewdrop form the sky.
In service high with the sweetness through the ears,
Bring all Paradise before the eyes.
Let that service be in conformity with God's purpose.

Service, the backbone of human life it is;
Makes us selfless as we work for God and others;
As in the acts done with the intention of
Devoting ourselves altogether to God;
As in performance of official or professional duties;
As in a religious rite appropriate to a particular event,
Or a form followed in worship or in ceremony;
As in the habit or practice of serving God;
And as heart fully as these core,
With a service guided by love,
Rightfully will our action be.
Demonstrate to God that he is worthy;
Serve him by giving yourself to him;
Serve others and put your own interest aside;
Serve him with a servant's spirit,
Execute your deeds with compassion.
Serve him with the expectation of nothing in return;
Serve him for who he is; and
Serve him with a humble and obedient spirit.
With the right service, abundantly will our reward be.

FEAR

<u>**AFFILIATED QUOTE:**</u>

"Throughout my spiritual development, my fear of the Lord increased as I learned more about the attributes of the Almighty God. With my knowledge, I humbly respect and reverence God for his holiness, righteousness, majesty, and power".

Fear

Not much knowest, but thou exist;
What hell it is celebrating the possession of thy victim?
God days to lose that might be better spent;
Long night to waste in costly discontent;
To cheat on hope;
To pine in fear; To drill in sorrow;
To engulf thy heart with comfortless despair;
Unhappy wit in weak, frail, disease, instability,
War, terrorism, and pollution;
To disastrous end they are born.
The dark shadow, the shadow itself;
Spreading within thyself,
Caging us and ultimately imprison within ourselves.
The enemy to mankind it is;
Stumbling block to progress it is;
Deterrent it is from achieving intended objectives and goals.
Dark shadow how persistent and detrimental can you be?
Mankind's stability you tend to block?
Worry not for the ultimate solution is in within.
Admit the fear;
Focus on the fear;
Face the fear head-on;
Disregard the fear as powerful;
Now, along the way,
Stand beside healthy trees through thick and thin adventures.
The antidote of fear and the wonder neutralizer,
Think more of love;
Love expels all fear and a normal lifestyle is granted.

Not much knowest, there is brightness that comes
With the rising of the sun;
There is hope in the shining of the stars;
There is a teacher, the fear instructor;
The fear of the Lord it is.
With it, implied is respect, obedience, humility,
And reverence for God;
Introducing and recognizing God's attributes:
Holy he is;
Pure he is;

Righteous he is;
Omnipotent he is;
Omniscient he is;
Omnipresent he is.
In his image as created,
A clearer picture of ourselves we gain.
Though distance away,
For unexpectedly, on our way,
May arrive with special opportunities;
Commencing the starting point of a mindset of faith,
Real wisdom we find.
As we look on to God,
Troubles appear not disappear;
But, less frighten they become as rearranged and
With God directing our thoughts, words,
And deeds bolted with the right perspective we are.
The antidote of fear,
God's presence you recognize.
To supply you with courage, confidence,
And resources at the right moment trust God.

Not much knowest, but, phobia it sometimes becomes;
It sails on strong and great,
Breathlessly on thy fate, you hang.
Penetrating on us, there is shadow at the rising of the sun;
Melting us at dawn, there is shadow in the rising of the moon;
Nature the teacher will show us something different from either.
The shadow among us;
The shadow surrounding us;
The shadow under the "granite slab".
The trees give no shelter,
The rain with no relief neither.
A heap of broken images,
Where the sun, the moon hit;
But still no relief, but in the mind;
For distilled almost to jelly is this act;
That fear itself is the only thing to be afraid of.
Face it. For no coward soul,
No trembler can stand when Heaven's glory shines.
This condition,
That condition is neither natural between anxiety and terror;
Among us, well-grounded they are.
Brave it is to face it;

Brave it is to stay put with a shivering soul;
Brave it is to overcome that trailing monster.
For neutralized and effective, we stay with bold composure.
With his power and might,
God is our shelter and hiding place.
From our heart, inappropriate fear he will drive.
Only fear is fear to itself, with love, incinerated it is.

CHARACTERS

<u>**AFFILIATED QUOTE:**</u>

"As I always state, the best ways to define myself are those particular moral attitudes that are deeply and intensely active within me. No one can define my inner self, except God and me".

Characters

Oh what a world,
The celebrities rich and famous as role models;
Termites they are; contaminants they are;
The minds of fans they contaminate,
Upon the globe, hell they bestow with avarice.
Like parasites, they are all over,
Their host they eat up from in within.
The minds of fans travel the wrong direction,
Porcine become the termites.
Like mirage, they habitually design the fans' characters;
As the minds of the fans go the wrong direction,
So nourished become the termites.
Now the so-called acceptable customs:
Possessions, types of relationship, ways to communicate,
Ways to dress, ideal shapes and sizes;
They are the Lucifer of the world;
They are the core of acceptance;
Distance becomes the sheep from God.
Now the worst of hell is on earth;
Pathetic fallacy they produce:
Impressions of things are in falsehood.
With state of mind aggressively contaminated,
Negative attributes are produced,
Saturating societal ethics with destructive epidemic;
The condition full of falsehood of uncertainty:
Chaos, greed, pride, selfishness, depression, and grief;
The artificial role models, you must change;
The real role models, you must adopt;
God the ultimate role model, his ways you follow.
The perfect and distinguish model he is;
With perfect attributes, the right role model is God.
With humble submission,
Follow the traits of God's characters.

There is no straight path;
It is all existing contrary to what was once an acceptable core.
Without moral values
The society flourishes with negative attributes,
Like a river, it flows.
Contaminated is the society with low class disrespectful values.

No respect for one another;
No respect for the elders;
Family relationship in disarray;
No respect for divinity.
A man-made hallucination is the name of God perceived.
Disobedience is the way of life.
Destroyer of societal values,
Destructive attributes they are fatly from societal fallacy.
Look at you,
You want to be in control all the time.
Who do you think you are?
Look at that,
Always self-pitiful you are;
Stubbornness you continuously exhibit;
Full of defective characters you are;
Upon you, shame, shame.
Watch out, laziness to the defects you are inviting.
Hurt will these defects cause in you;
Remove them just for one day at a time.
For God judge not by appearance,
By faith, deed, and characters he does.
Humbly surrender to God and you shall be cleansed,
Purged, and developed.
Only available to God and yourself,
Is the knowledge of attributes of your heart.
Now with God in your life,
Developed and acceptable will your characters be.

PATIENCE

<u>AFFILIATED QUOTE:</u>

"Patience gives birth to the theory of "think before you act" into play; as it is now part of taking in a deep breath and expel it as your timer. Waiting in the rain is preferable as it calms you as you proceed steadfastly".

Patience

You keep searching, looking for the right action.
Keep strong, keep cool, keep relax;
Abode in the clouds with no disturbance,
With no distraction insight,
None essential becomes time.
Slide to the ocean,
Enjoy the soothing melody of the waves;
With a split of the light,
Time zooms as unexpectedly perceived;
Perseverance increases,
Endurance increases,
Expectation gets nearer, and
The exerted steadfastness pays off.
Like marriages from which love has gone,
Lacking patience nourishes divorce.
Like a frog, with patience everywhere,
Room for reconciliation, exist always.
Explore the appropriate option, God's spice;
Patience, the right ingredient, you choose to spice your arena.

With the armor of God you stand erected;
Armed with a heavy offensive weapon,
Patience with the multi-facet ingredients:
The highest value of uncertainty it is;
The best remedy for controversy it is;
The adversity of enduring adversity and pain with fortitude it is;
The steadfastness with self-possession in facing obstacles it is;
With integrity, we are clothed;
As waiting is patience;
Patience is waiting;
Waiting enhances endurance;
Endurance nourishes patience;
Patience is God's manna to the soul;
Our emotional state of mind, it satisfies;
The key to surviving prosecution, trial and trouble it is;
God in us, it generates to the glory of God.
With our faith and patience in God's action,
Perfect stays his timing in relieving our suffering,
Patiently wait on the Lord, for victorious it is always.

Bright star it is as transformed into steadfastness.
Now come the still of the night,
Forgetting all of times, it is with twilight gray.
Conversing like sleepless
Hermit, all change, all seasons;
As created in perception, look new.
Strong, cool and relax it is,
As with patience, the flame burns out.
Just as with ignorance,
Expelling thought of thy heart in the absence of thinking,
Whether too little,
Whether too much,
Chaotic without passion it is;
As partners and strongest of all warriors,
Time and patience co-exist, unfolding
With plight cunning hides as time exists.
Time, the essence and pattern of all patience,
Illuminate patience with light;
To thy soul, hidden treasure it is;
To thy heart, possessions it is.

Keep cool; keep strong;
Now the right spice you are familiar with;
Patience is flourishing among those who embraced it;
It renders the answer for many obstacles.
With the multifaceted qualities it encompasses,
No is anger, no is vexation exists where patience is present.
For under stress, provocation and indignity,
Patience flourishes with forbearance.
The birthplace of "think before you act" theory it is;
The composure under suffering
As in waiting for an unduly delayed outcome, it is.
Wherein, now into existence,
Is the remedy for unintended words and actions.
Let the patience of God, reflect into you;
For a waiting period is part of the fulfillment of his promise.
Adopt God's patience;
In strengthening, perseverance and character it is helpful.
Patience the wonder of mankind's consciousness;
Will flourish, where its presence is activated.

ENCOURAGEMENT

AFFILIATED QUOTE:

"Just tell someone who has failed in an endeavor that it is okay to fail. Tell them to re-evaluate the circumstance and try again. Tell them that they are good enough to be successful the next time around".

Encouragement

Seek support,
Clothe thyself with encouragement, inspiration and endurance.
The armor, put on;
The challenges, be set and ready;
The excess weight that deters your path, take off;
The race that God has set for you, run.
Like champion athletes you become;
Resilience, endurance, and strength you build through hard work.
Those negative baggage, strip off.
Motivation now surrounds thee as
Positive baggage committed to the race, now is the core.
To the race,
Drop-off certain activities;
Certain associates;
Certain affiliates;
Evaluate your standing;
Encouragement, the helping tool that inspire and help, gain;
To the finish line, you push through the pain and suffering;
With the new found inspiration, the race you finish.
Spiritually, secularly, traditionally
In nature they are the concepts in triplet association:
Encouragement, inspiration and support.
Horizontally, they operate;
Unified they are with
The main ingredients nourishing relationship,
To clothe circumstance not stored in a freezer.
Only in flashes,
Inspiration descends with encouragement.
Through God's purpose by prophetic voices of advice;
The action is to "spice-up the soup" for his people,
Just to continue the race to the finish line.

Oh encouragement,
How helpful and consoling you are?
A booster to the spirit you are;
A life corrector you are;
Attach thyself unto thee.
Purge me now?
Five feet away cannot be viewed.
I am lost, I am collapsing;

Failure is becoming my trend.
Cleanse me?
Boost me with motivation and perseverance.
Now with open eyes,
I can see with sight converging to a new view.
The detours divert to a straight paths;
The clouds are vanishing; and
The sunlight once more can be viewed.
Dropping out of the race,
Is no more part of the discussion.
Now actively I am part of the race;
With the new perception, new perspectives,
A new route is set;
Amended goals with new plans are set.
The consciousness is now
Engulfed with positive attitudes;
A rejuvenated creature,
One with inspiration, motivation, and
Hope has been set free;
To grab any opportunity on the path,
As I explore the sphere.
With encouragement now implanted in me,
A new creature I become pursuing my goals.

Lost will you be with the absence of encouragement;
Nothing seems to be in sight;
Ghostly remains the city as the search goes on;
You look for a Samaritan to boost-up the spirit.
Where are you?
In the midst of turmoil
Inspired and encouraged you stay
With knowledge that God is in control;
Be joyful, be relaxed, and be cool.
The lost ones,
Through awareness of God's attributes, encourage them;
The weak, through love and prayer, encourage them;
The timid, through reminder of God's promises, encourage them;
The obedient, through spreading the word of God, encourage them;
The depressed, through awareness of the love,
Consoling spirit and compassion of God, encourage them.
In so doing, others are built with God's love.
Ups and downs, in the globe, dominant forces they are.
To inspire and support others,

The wanted list spread around in search for principles.
Begin with encouragement;
Expect of yourself what you expect from others.
With consideration, develop the expectation;
Lead and monitor the expectation;
Extending thanks you end up with.
With inconvenience,
With conformability not,
No matter what format it is,
Whatever status the task may seem, the race still goes on;
The support you seek to stimulate, inspire
And encourage to finishing the race.

RELIGION

<u>**AFFILIATED QUOTE:**</u>

"My personal commitment to God is to serve him with my conduct and devotion in accordance with his commands. For religion is deep within me; my perception, my ideology, my faith, and the consoling spirit within me. All in one that gives me hope and comfort in times of devastation".

Religion

There it goes, the parade just started;
Into existence mankind now on earth,
Flying with the winy mysteries in divinity;
The airy subtleties in a belief system;
On which directed are all the reason and conviction;
Violence not,
Force not, mankind, by such,
By dictate of conscience,
Equally entitled to, is the free exercise of religion.
As such, mentality has hinged within the brains for better
Conviction of the existence of a supreme being,
That being, special he is with unimaginable influence.
Devotion, in multiple shapes and forms it exist.
In the Almighty God only, some are devoted;
In the Almighty God, the Son and the Holy Spirit,
Some are devoted;
In just any god, some are devoted;
In an evil god, some are devoted;
In multiples gods, some are devoted;
In science and human intuition, some are devoted;
In none existence of gods, some are devoted.
Not matter what and who,
It is all a system of faith and worship;
With perceptive mind that inspire zealous devotion.
In accordance with God's commandment and purpose;
In worshipful devotion and conduct,
Personal choice it is to serve God Almighty.
By grace and salvation, we live;
In humility and obedience, we are restored;
Restore we are to the dignity of God;
Devoting and venerating the majesty of God.

Flowing like lava,
Speedily religion spread all over.
The feeling, the perception, the attitude;
Magnanimity it is;
As a verity,
As any other part of human consciousness;
Flowing deep into the inner calling of mankind,
Generating faith the beget heretics.

As the mind grows, so expanded it becomes;
So spread like grass spots it becomes;
By our actions, controlled it can be, or
Uncontrolled it can spread.
With materialism as the main core of society lifestyle,
Multi-facet shapes and forms of devotion are now incorporated.
As superstition, some are devoted;
As false prophets, some are devoted;
As a way to gain fame, some are devoted;
As a way to manipulate others, some are devoted;
As the road to riches, some are devoted.
It is not just a system of faith and worship,
Deeper it is than the outward exhibition;
A system of business venture with worldliness
As the main objective and to
Generate self-contentment in inspiring zealous devotion.
By so centered,
The conciliation of supernatural powers,
Used directly to control human activity and to
Establish a core of acceptable practice.
By the mind-set, by lack of faith,
Limit not the powers of the Almighty God;
For by the actions and attitudes, God judges all.

REPENTANCE

<u>AFFILIATED QUOTE:</u>

"It was all about me. It doesn't matter how I get it; all that
matter is that, I get it. Selfishness is my core game.
The more money I get, the more I seek.
I desire to be the most famous. I seek influence.
I enjoyed women, night clubs, alcohol, and nasty attitudes were
chores of my choice. Never was good intention within me
until when I almost lost all my fortune.
Then, I realized there's a Higher Power who controls
everything. With good intentions, I confessed and asked
for forgiveness of my sins".

Repentance

Adopt the mainstream garbage;
Breathe the world's thought;
Copyright the disgusting lifestyle;
Do the world's deeds;
Famous it is, great it is;
Life becomes a light;
Illuminable is this light, brighter than daytime light.
Disobedience is now part of life;
Selfishness, self-centeredness now core of the so-called,
The greatest of them all:
Multiple girlfriends, extra-marital affairs,
Alcohol consumption, swearing, profanities, and
Most acts contradictory to God's commands.
Those excitements, those blunders are now part of miseries,
That set forth discontent in within;
Within the atmosphere, fling forth, is sorrow.
The attitude, the behavior unimaginable it is,
Beyond societal expectation it saturates.
In sin, you swim;
In disgust, you thrive;
In restlessness, you bathe; In insomnia, you rest;
In unhappiness, you abide;
In distress, reality knocks at the entrance.
Full responsibility you take as you repent and
Confess to the Almighty God;
With patience, you now wait for God to act.

The barrel is full,
In the fire of winter,
Fling is the garment of repentance.
The repentance, the confession,
For the worse you have done,
Not much regret is in within;
But the fear as to the consequences of the trouble,
That flows within you.
The moment is here,
Grab it before it is ripe;
To wipe off the tears of repentance,
The moment is ripe, ready for harvest.
In awareness of the sins,

In willingness you confess genuinely,
And petition for guidance to turn away from sins.
God's guidance you seek to gain God's attention;
Your attitude and lifestyle, you discern;
Your peers and associates, you discern,
The sins in your life, you extinguish;
To know God better, about God, you learn;
Your life, you live in accordance with God's commandment.
Now rejuvenated you are
With a moral and spiritual correct life;
With a personal relationship with God;
With obedience and trust in God;
Flowing like milk and honey,
Be the forgiveness of sins.

In the religiously proclaimed,
Abode is the parasite, hypocrisy;
Be not that devout religious person who
Traps repentance during Sunday worship
For sinful acts done on Saturday,
Combined with what sinful acts will be done on Monday.
Mere lip-service it is;
For with words of confession,
In conjunction with acts to abstain from sinful lifestyle,
True repentance comes with being truly sorry.
Like a vaccine for a disease;
It won't help unless it enters the bloodstream;
So be repentance and confession;
Accepted not by God,
Unless made with remorsefulness, and
Inwardly, guaranteed with true intention.
Cover with guilt,
The shame you hide not from every eye;
With dedication of oneself,
To the abandonment of unwanted purpose and value;
With the realization of the source of sins;
With the vital confession of sin;
With honest surrender to God;
With complete and instant obedience;
With faithfulness and humility to God;
So be the ingredients of reconciliation and redemption,
As they spring up a true religious life.

REPUTATION

<u>**AFFILIATED QUOTE:**</u>

"Some of us claim how we live our life is our own prerogative;
so we forge a reputation by developing qualities by which
people will remember us for. We should always remember that
God judges us by our deeds today for our
salvation and eternal life".

Reputation

There they are;
The oceans, the rivers, the plains,
The hills, the valleys;
All in consistent display of cores though differ but,
Agree with their known reaction to nature,
As nature knocks at their entrance,
Each demonstrates their revealed reputation.
Oh, see how defiant you sit?
As your own prerogative,
You equate that proclaimed way of life.
For yourself, you establish personal qualities to be remembered.
Consistently, you work hard, kind, loving, self-centeredness,
And cooperative; the qualities of life you believe in.
United you are wherever you are with these qualities;
Whatever you do reflects these qualities;
Judge not by God are the
Achievements, credentials, and accomplishments;
No matter how impressive they appear to be.
For your reputation determines your eternal life,
Whatever deed is executed, God takes notes.

Look at that,
So humble, befriending everyone;
You move around with your head upright;
Through the city you are cruising to help the needy and poor;
Words of inspiration, you render;
Words of courage, you expel;
Words of motivation, you preach;
In your entire endeavor, consistent at every moment
You are with encouragement.
As you gain the reputation in fulfilling their day's expectation,
People wait for your arrival.
The eyes see; the heart evaluate;
Now with good reputation, you are renowned;
The Samaritan you are as atmospherically you shine.
For promised eternal life in Paradise, accepted you will be;
Not for your achievements,
But, for the good deeds executed during your lifetime,
And the godly ways you treat the needy and depressed.
With a good reputation among the people,
Righteously, you live in peace and harmony.

PRAYER

<u>AFFILIATED QUOTE:</u>

"In humble submission pray to the Almighty God. He is there waiting for your petition. In daily devotion, I submit this prayer to God Almighty:

As I arise today, I praise you Almighty God for your majesty, power, and might. I thank you for this life that you breathe in me to wake me up in health and in strength. Please Father Almighty, forgive me from the sins that I have committed, known and unknown. Bring me closer to you.

In my continuous life, may the strength and power of God Almighty pilot and uphold. May God grant me wisdom and knowledge; may God protect my family and me from all visible and invisible enemies; may God pilot my family to be devout and dedicated religious family; may the grace and peace of God that surpasses all grace and peace be bestowed upon my family and me, amen".

Prayer

To express the motion of a hidden fire,
From within it trembles;
To express thy soul's sincere desires,
To boost thy soul by tender stroke of devotion;
To develop an obedient attitude;
The heart you cleanse from contamination.
All action is established within a conscious virtue bold.
Equate over each scene;
Live over each scene;
Transform to what they behold;
For every situation,
Willingly you are to turn to Higher Power for solution.
Systematic and organized is God;
So in reaching him,
Your thoughts, preparation,
Effort and planning should be organized.
With praise, thanksgiving, repentance, commitment,
And special requests you come to the Lord.
As prayers are expressed,
Clarified and effective they become;
Responsibility of what to do is acknowledged;
With the knowledge that God has the great power to help,
With time, a strong relationship with him is cultivated.
The art of praying you explore;
With time, faith, trust, and obedience,
Prayer will be amalgamated as part of your daily activity.

Oh conscience, upright and stainless,
Spilling out thy heart's desire;
Progress as directed with a solemn and
Humble approach to Divinity;
Hitches up-beat formula of supplication,
Ride smoothly into confession and petition,
Relax with great expectation;
The moment is it that the "host of Heaven doth chime".
With wisdom, understanding, fortitude,
Patience, peace, joy, modesty, and fidelity,
In calm retreat with the day of consoling truth, the soul rests.
Peep into your portfolio;

Is there a need for adjustment?
Analyze and re-arrange carefully;
Are your priorities in order?
With such evaluation,
If to no avail, complaint not about the problem;
For prayer, the fault terminator, once adopted,
The answer you sort will be displayed.
When praying,
Be not in the regular posture;
In humble submission you must come before God.
When you come, come if possible by
Prostrating, kneeling, or bowing with eyes closed;
With a clear conscience and concentration;
Inferiority to God is established.

Look at that, just sitting waiting to snatch a victim.
Do you think you can curtail thy feeling to pray?
You can embed guilty feelings within?
You cannot block the only available means of restoration?
Praying, you must do.
Oh temptation, how weak you've become with his prayers.
For with prayers,
Strengthen is he to resist even the force of a tornado.
In desperation, you have done it;
Now pacing around all impatient you are,
A spontaneous response you expect.
Relax, be patient;
For steadfastly you should stay.
If years have passed by, do not despair.
For not always in harmony,
Not by the expectation,
For in accordance to his perspectives,
For what is good for us,
The mighty one answers.
With truthful submission and faith,
Comfort we feel;
Assurance we obtain;
On an unexpected day,
Milk and honey will pour down from the sky.
Pray, God is with us all the time;
Trust him and wait patiently.

With expectation,
The father waits for petitions from his children.
In like manner, God patiently wait for thy petition.
Prayer, the key to reach God,
Upon thy inner core, bestows a comfortable rest.
Prayer, faith, and hope working side by side,
Triplet they are;
When negative energy encompasses thee;
When faith begins to fail;
When hope begins to decline;
When thinking and comprehension abandoned;
When all alone;
When all effort in vain;
With tears running down, to the rescue machine you turn;
Pray, pray, and pray;
Keep on praying.
The prayer machine, the wagon to the land of solution;
An exhibit with a clear picture will it renders you.
Never perceive you are abandoned;
Never perceive that God is silent unnecessary;
Never perceive that God is aboding far away from you;
For God hears and evaluate your prayers silently and privately.
As you pray, proclaim fulfillment of thy desire;
Proclaim fulfillment of your petition;
For somewhere, sometimes,
The special delivery will come thy way.

PRAISE

AFFILIATED QUOTE:

"As you open your eyes praise and thank the Almighty God for breathing life into you and for waking you in health and in strength. As we praise, re-clothe we are in our right mind, moving from the physical sphere to the spiritual sphere. Praise focuses our attention on God and reminds us of God's attributes. So, all God's creatures great and feeble praise him and receive his love and the power of the Holy Spirit. Praise God to exhibit your appreciation as he forgives your sins; heals your illnesses; redeems you from death to eternal life; gives righteous judgment; and grants your heart's desire".

Praise

Again, you must become an ignorant man;
Again, with an ignorant eye you see the sun.
In the idea of it, see it clearly,
For praise is the only thing you want as you ask for criticism.
Forget not the last right opinion;
For the first opinion, you review.
So some praise you extend at the morning watch;
For what is blamed at the night watch.
Enough it is to have determination;
For when strength fails,
Boldness will certainly win praise.
If ever give praise not; if ever experience disgrace not;
Spring out of existence is miserable state of mind,
Produced by the wretched soul;
In disarray and distress, your status is.
It glows in every heart, reigns in every soul, refines in every attitude;
As the love of praise re-clothe thee in thy rightful mind;
With purer lives by thy service you are established;
In deeper reference to a superior being,
Shining in the sky, as he, according to his perspectives,
Your heart's desire, he will deliver.
It might not be according to thy timetable;
It might not be according to thy expectation;
But, in praise and special petition,
It will happen with patience and steadfastness.
Special delivery will someday,
Sometimes arrive at thy doorstep.

Again, it is implanted, always harvested;
Again, to be in the world of ups and downs,
Lays within mankind for positive effect on attitude,
For spiritual celebration, it is the greatest outlet;
Available it is for no charge but, from self-will.
As in expressing commendation for an act well done;
As in expressing to God our appreciation
And understanding for his excellence;
As in expressing ourselves in worshipping by song,
Dancing, or with musical instruments as
Distinguish from prayers and other acts;
As in expressing ourselves when our inward feeling

Becomes our outward expression;
As in expressing ourselves in helping ourselves with an
Increased knowledge and awareness of God;
As in focusing our hearts and entire concentration on God;
As in expressing ourselves by saying thanks to
God for the attributes of his majestic Divinity;
So be the aspects of praise.
Transforming from the physical realm to the spiritual realm,
Situated you are in the right form of
Mind as you praise God first,
Then earnestly submit your petition to him.
So do not wait for winning-praise of others;
For your heart cleanses from praising God;
Station with clarity and confidence,
Distance from distraction you will abode.

Again, thy ears must have been opened;
Again, experience must have taught thee
The significant of the star-like action, praise.
Now you know how;
Whatever is fickle?
Whatever is freckled?
Whether dazzle, whether slow, whether sweet,
Whether bitter, whether chaotic, whether stagnant;
Constantly stays the Supreme God,
Always praise him from within.
With hands extended,
Willingly he gives audience to thy praise and petition.
Forgiving our sin, he does;
Healing our diseases, he does;
Comforting and consoling, he does;
Bestowing wisdom, knowledge, and understanding, he does;
Giving righteous judgment, he does;
Crowning us with compassion and love, he does;
Granting our hearts' desires, he does.
With such multi-facet attributes,
Praise him and count thy blessing daily.
With praise, problems and shortcomings dissipate;
Perspectives are transformed from physical to spiritual;
God majestic attributed are appreciated;
To receive God's blessings,
Hearts are conditioned to focus.
All creatures on earth, praise God Almighty.

PERSECUTION

<u>**AFFILIATED QUOTE:**</u>

"The only object, subject, and effect of persecution is persecution itself. For Contrary to the intended purpose, unexpected consequences are generated.

For persecution is the by-product of envy, jealousy, bitterness, arrogance, and selfishness. If persecuted for your religious belief, be proud, be thankful to God. When you steadfastly stay, God will reward you abundantly.

If persecuted because of your race or complexion, be proud because the persecutor is jealous and wants to be like you. In any persecution, be strong, be steadfast, and hold on to what you believe in and who you are".

Persecution

For God I live;
Faithfully I proclaim his message.
A nice day it is,
A quiet day it is,
A favored day, the vicinity you stroll.
It is a sound,,,,,,,,,,
I hear the voice.
It sounds like when Jesus said "Saul, Saul,
Why are you persecuting me?"
It echoes and echoes, and echoes;
It keeps on going.
Centered I am in my prerogative just taking care of business.
In a split of a sound,
From nowhere came a raging bull,
Heading to my direction,
Charging full speed without provocation;
Determined to consume me;
From every angle, it charges.
A campaign well planned to extirpate my faith.
Energized I am,
Strengthen becomes my faith,
To keep on spreading the message,
Fueled I am with endurance, courage, and determination.
The suffering, the imprisonment, the humiliation,
The irritation, the threat, the torture, the scandal;
All welcome as a victory march in spreading the message.
In spite of all persecution,
If steadfastly faithful you stay;
For spiritually, suffer not;
For eternally, loss not;
For when darkness befalls thee,
Thou no more,
Wrapped all around me by God,
Is the grand prize, eternal life.

Overshadow by darkness,
As some thrive with the fruit of wickedness,
Satanic becomes the world.
Perspectives, embossed and adherent in several stain glasses,

Contaminating the flocks:
Some welcome God;
Some reject God;
Some just reject everything, anything.
For their tradition,
For their deed,
For their belief,
For their faith,
Christians have been persecuted;
Christian Scientists have been persecuted;
Jews have been persecuted;
Muslims have been persecuted;
Buddhists have been persecuted;
Atheists have been persecuted; and
Tribally and racially you have been persecuted.
With persecution, steadfastly holding on your grounds,
Borne is the opportunity to educate the predators and
Gain free help in witnessing to most.
You may be ridiculed;
You may be ostracized;
You may be slandered;
You may be imprisoned;
You may be beaten;
You may be scorned;
You may be killed.
In spite of the threats, frighten not, all that matters,
Sharing ideas, perspectives, belief or faith,
You will be transformed by sliding forward.
Joyous will you feel and
Showers of blessing will pour down from heaven.

Quivering not in the world's storm evil sphere;
By my deeds, heaven's glory shine I seek.
At whatever cost,
Whatever threats, and
Whatever humiliation:
Determined I am in witnessing for God.
Places that are less barbaric, smooth,
Or clear I look for; and
Speak of those to rest my weary ear. In unity,
Persecution and witnessing live together as host and parasite.
With an opportunity to spread God's word,

Persecution nourishes witnessing.
Beneficial is it to the Kingdom of God
When sufferers of persecution are
United in God as brothers and sisters;
When they suffer, the entire community suffers.
Just like the human body,
When one part suffers,
The whole body suffers.
But when all parts are united and coordinated
As one to fight the problem,
Ease up becomes the pain and suffering.
Red carpet not,
Guarantee not from persecution;
Though with faithfulness in witnessing;
For God warrants character enhancement,
Guidance, direction, endurance, strength and
Perseverance with rewards of recognition,
Grace, salvation, and eternal life.
In spite of the religious, social,
Political or economic persecution,
God's ministry flourishes continuously.

SHINING ARMOR AND I, INSEPARABLE AND TOGETHER
<u>AFFILIATED QUOTE:</u>

"She is around; the feeling comes from in within. I experience it, I feel it. She is all around my sphere. There is not a day without her dominating spirit with me".

Shining Armor and I, Inseparable and Together

I long for her,
I stretch for her,
The alarm cord, I pull for her.
As I lift my amber beam that fell aslant,
There shine the beauty of Shining Armor
As embossed with the three parallel colors:
Nothing but white, white, and white.
Loving and kind be one;
Compassionate and reasonable be one; and
Trustworthy and truthful is one.
Her attributes are so perfect that recharged
Becomes my charisma just with the
Glimpse of her enticing smile.
Excitedly, I operate with her beauty before me;
The beauty behind me;
The beauty above me;
The beauty below me;
The beauty all over me; and
The beauty is in within me.
As long as the moon shall rise;
As long as the stars shall dazzle;
As long as the sun shall shine;
Our union with everlasting energy will sparkle,
Generating acclaimed charisma revived within me.
A woman so renowned and powerful,
On her domain she sits,
All over the world of faith, she establishes me.
In contentment, we live in each other;
In ecstasy, we love each other;
As inseparably, united we are;
Adhesively, we are amalgamated.

I experience life with her;
I develop characters with her;
Toward God's path,
I successfully move with her.
With sanctification and blessing from Higher Power,
A relationship from Paradise is borne;
Springing forth the object of nature,

With inspiration, that formulates my mortal frame.
Flowing from Paradise,
Through the sky into my inner core;
All passion, all ecstasies,
All delights, all thoughts, and all energies;
Components they are with nutritious compounds,
Fills up my barrel,
As extracted from Shining Armor.
A bouquet of love, she brings to me;
A bow of smelting gold,
She brings to me; arrow of fulfillment,
She brings to me;
Spears of adventure, she brings to me; and
Chariot of confidence, she brings to me.
With Shining Armor, a complete package I am.
The sweet thoughts that saturate me;
The thought of love that engulfed me;
All around, Shining Armor is all over me.
The love that kindles my gentle heart in a fair form,
Seize me so strongly;
As inseparably, we are;
Adhesively, we are together.

SEASONS

AFFILIATED QUOTE:

"By nature, seasons affect every living creature. There are seasons for everything; even the moon, stars, and sun all with their assigned seasons.
God is reminding us that certain things are beyond our control. So we should learn to accept that we cannot change and change things that we have control over".

Seasons

The seasons, the weather, and matter
All intermingle on an ongoing process.
Time brings forth the hurricane seasons;
Time brings forth the tornado seasons;
Time brings forth the cold seasons;
Time brings forth the hot seasons; and
Time brings forth the moderate seasons.
Oh seasons, how gracious you are?
Mankind prepares and plans for what
Circumstance is perceived, with experience.
By the seasons of delight:
Winter, spring, summer, and autumn are exposed.
The wrathful nipping cold of the barren winter,
With drear attitude, is introduced with layers of garments.
This introduces the passage to the chill and doleful atmosphere.
Old man winter brings forth the rain of spring.
Plants, flowers sprung out alerting of springtime;
The rain pours down reminding us of a change of attitude.
Spring calls forth summer warmth.
Summer has the brightest, longest days with energies.
Vibrant, merry, lively with charisma is the atmosphere.
Summer changes mood;
It caves into the fading period of the cool of autumn.
With autumn, of humans, of animals, of herds, of trees;
For what is ahead, the preparation they commence.
Honey to you should all the seasons be.
Whether be winter, spring, summer or autumn,
Welcome should be all with joyous heart as time passes by.

For all matter, there are seasons;
With his might, into existence they are conferred.
Seasons and time, time and seasons;
All in collaboration, nature mortal core they are.
All nature seems to work.
Lovely, see the cloud, the cloud appears;
Lovely, see the rain, the rain pours down;
Change of seasons, change of time;
For the energetic era, you sound the bell.
Generation and generation are exhibited
To the clan as newborns are introduced.

All the charm and excitement flow.
Seasons, through metamorphism,
Transform rocks into all shapes, sizes and colors;
Soft to hard, hard to soft;
Seasons cause the sharpest of sword to rust and deform;
Even the strongest of metals decay.
Into everlasting darkness, delivers the healthiest creatures.
Seasons oh seasons; thou produce and thou take.
What can the mortal soul imply?
Nothing, but unto nature they surrender.
Into existence, by nature they are;
Seasons of connection of man and woman, animals and mammals;
Seasons of joy and sorrows;
Seasons of dismay, fall, trouble, love, rise and excitements;
Seasons of receiving and giving;
Seasons of maladies, seasons of everlasting darkness.
A world of unpredictability so complex, merge as one.

AUTUMN

AFFILIATED QUOTE:

"Nature is in control. It gives us the seasons. At will, it can change the seasons according to its perspective. Autumn is the preparation icon".

AUTUMN

Sitting between hot and cold, here comes the moderator;
It is autumn.
Autumn is here; the cooling machine, you turn on.
Embrace what nature has in store for us.
The clouds hang oppressively low in the
Sky as the days start to shrink;
The nights start to expand;
In the battle, the sunshine start losing its steam
As the chill gains dominancy.
As September surrenders to October,
The chills remind us that autumn has arrived.
The day sky is chill;
The night sky brings more chill and doleful.
The earth's creatures prepare for the harsh condition ahead.
The season of relocation, specialized construction, and
Handyman workmanship has arrived:
Birds' nests, animal shelters, hibernation shelters,
Fine-tuning of home heating systems;
For the sleeping era ahead, preparation for survival it is.
October leaves are brown red or brown, sear and fall in wind.
October molds trees with protective blankets;
Balded become the stems and branches,
As shredded become the leaves.
In eyeing at the autumn fields,
As the thoughts of energies are encompassed,
Gradually dissipating are the excitement and vibrant countenance.
Like a clock with weak batteries,
The wheels of nature though fading,
Still stand with confidence.
It doesn't matter what mankind does,
Nature and seasons will always interplay.

WINTER

"Sitting by the fireplace as I enjoy the glow of the firewood, for the sullen and sad rule of winter I wait. To some it is delightful, to others it is dreadful; the subject of debate it is".

Winter

Winter, the mother of spring,
The offspring of autumn;
How smooth is your Introduction with the coldest period?
Stamped you are with less activities,
Dreariness and extended rest time.
Overshadow, be the daytime sunshine by the strength of your cold.
Overshadow, be the nighttime moon rise by the clouds.
You bring us small tabular columnar white crystals of frozen water;
The vicinity you transform to white;
For outdoor cold lovers
As you make available multiple recreational sports,
Gifts of paradise you establish for them.
Winter oh reputable one,
Delightful you are in harmonious homes;
During the day, the sunshine is mostly oblique.
As the cold flexes her muscles through,
In multiple layers of fabrics become the style;
Mankind bundles-up to cruise the atmosphere.
During the whole of a dull, dark, and soundless day in the winter;
Deep into that darkness peering,
As you doubt,
You wonder,
You dream,
You recollect;
As slow-down perspectives become prevalent,
A melancholic attitude is generated in thee,
Just like a load is dropped on you.
Barren winter with her wrathful nipping cold;
Marks she always deposit wherever her presence is felt:
Cruel and fierce storms,
Sharp and violent, dangerous to travel,
Potholes, accidents, traffic jams, road closures;
The ruler of inverted period,
Mayhem you are with your presence;
How dreadful can you be at your choosing?
In all we know,
Nature is at work with its own agenda.

SUMMER

<u>**AFFILIATED QUOTE:**</u>

"Summer, the season of jubilation, excitement, energy, merry
brings even the smallest of creatures to vibrant charisma.
The brightest, warmest and longest days; earns the title as the
mood swinger".

Summer

Thou vibrant summer,
Full of fun,
Full of social activities,
Full of excitements,
The aggressive product of spring you are;
The forerunner of autumn you are;
As reckoned astronomically from June solstice to September equinox;
Characterized you are with the warmest sunshine,
Brightness of the day,
Joys, lushness, and delights; and
The longest days of energies,
Vigor, and vibrant charisma;
The mood changer within mankind's soul it is.
On the street, on the beach, and everywhere;
Uplifted spirit you generate;
Beauty flashes all around;
Fashioned clothes flash all around;
Well-contoured, out-of-contoured,
In all shapes and forms they appear flashing all around.
Nice is the scenery,
Encouraging is the scenery,
Entertaining is the scenery;
You eye, you grasp what's exhibited;
Multi-generations are out there enjoying the summer warmth.
The days of outdoor activities,
The days when multitudes stay outdoor;
Days when birds return to the vicinity;
These are the days when blue sky resumes;
These are the days when most couples get married;
These are the days when schools are on vacation; and
These are the days of swimming pools and beaches.
The time for entertainment,
The time for inclusion, and
The time for interaction;
What a time to
Enjoy the warmth of the summer sun.
Grateful are the trees, plants, and flowers
To exhibit their multi-facet colorful beauties,

As there is
No spring,
No winter,
No autumn,
Generate beautiful displays of elegance as that of the summer.
Nature with his authoritative rule,
Flexes his muscles in whatever way he chooses.

SPRING

<u>**AFFILIATED QUOTE:**</u>

"Regenerating, rejuvenating; so is spring as everything
begins again".

Spring

Spring oh spring,
You bring back balmy warmth;
Ancestor of summer you are;
Messenger of the favorable atmospheric pressure ahead you are;
A flourishing stage of development you are;
With your might,
You maintain the world
As the producer of the most rain of blessing;
Life enhancer for crops, plants, trees; and
For lake, creeks, brooks, rivers, dams and reservoirs,
Water supplier you are.
To the world,
To generate brighter outlook,
Resourceful and innovative you are.

Now it is springtime,
From afar and from all around,
The ringtones of singing birds can be heard.
The fragrance of colorful flowers can be sniffed from afar,
Insects and flowers flourish in germination;
Every day in the garden,
A hidden affair it is,
Full of surprises as bulbs transform into folded blade,
With artistic display, the ground is pierced;
Trees, once barren,
Now healthy with leaves;
Fruits sprout out.
Birds, animals introduce their newborns to the world;
Weed once grass, shallow-rooted, now dominate the yard.

Without the taste of winter's adversities,
Spring would not be so pleasant;
So rejuvenating is the theme for spring.
Everything begins again;
In the spring,
Baseball, the game of American's heart, begins.
Spring the season of ever-flowing water,
Blossoms fill the gardens;
As nature introduces its ingenuity to the world,

Rain, tornado, and thunderstorm fill the day and night.
With compassion,
Nature bestows spring upon the globe;
Spring the life sustainer,
For mankind's survival, supplies nutritious ingredients.

CRITICISM

AFFILIATED QUOTE:

"Criticism comes with various intentions. It can be beneficial, detrimental or even plain stupid. People may try to discourage you with mockery or intimidating comments.
Always remember the qualities they are condemning are within their character's fallacies.
In responding to criticism, stay calm, maintain your composure; either ignore it, or accept it if beneficial to you.
Abstain from unjustifiably criticizing others. Always evaluate your own log first before you count the quantity of specks in other's eyes".

Criticism

Gauging, as to the heart of mankind to go adrift of things;
Grace not,
Reason not,
Bow not to accept reality of the moment.
You watch to see if he is going to clean the pasture spring,
Or rake the leaves away,
Or watch the water clear.
Hesitation, he executes;
But, with criticism he continues.
Trifling is the disagreement;
The issue exists untouched.
You eye and detect the envy and pride,
From the real issue, you create a diversion.
Stop and question yourself,
Refusal you expel.
Instead, a smoke screen you created.
To face the real problem,
Afraid you are to address the continuous criticism.
React not to hurtful words;
For hope,
Exchange self-pity and dwell in the relationship with God.

Gauging, as to his intention;
It shows as if a night of dark intent is advancing.
For rage, he prepares;
The true intention, he conceals.
His own character flaws he cages;
Strategically, he trashes the qualities of others.
Unjustifiably the criticism is,
The abuse, quietly the victim tolerates.
With face upright in composure,
Determinably he holds to his posture.
Don't hear,
Don't see, is now the strategic action.
Trifling is the criticism
For consequential emotional drain,
Discouraged with negative mockery is the intention.
Again, as the unjustified criticism circle,
Quietly tolerant he becomes,
Composure he maintains.

Suddenly the judge realizes,
Indirectly looking at him in the mirror,
Is condemning others,

Gauging, as to good can the criticism be;
As to the wise and humble heart of mankind,
In a godly manner, constructive criticism is expressed.
Productive rather than destructive it is;
The by-product is helpful in realization;
With verified facts,
It is given with true intention.
Responsively for guidance with ears open attentively,
Silently to God Almighty, he prays.
Evaluate your own log,
After consideration of kindness;
What is right, you do;
The criticism, you accept.
Trifling, as to the sentiment and restlessness;
For valuable it becomes to reciprocate the sentiment;
To accumulate the qualities being ministered,
You penetrate to fish.
With persevering attitude,
Supply not the critics with ammunition;
For with rightful action executed,
Beneficial becomes the criticism.

DECISIONS IN SPIRITUAL SENSE

AFFILIATED QUOTE:

"In all significant decisions, I first seek God Almighty
wisdom and guidance; then, I utilize the basic principles
dealing with sound decisions:
Open to new ideas, I stay;
Carefully, I hear and evaluate both sides of the story; and I
get the facts together before making the decision.
Finally, I stand up for what is right no matter what others'
pressure me to do otherwise".

Decisions in Spiritual Sense

For freewill it is;
For it is all on your recreational ground;
You choose, you reject, the choice is yours.
You possess, you dispossess, your prerogative it is.
In your court is the ball;
It is no one else ball to play the game;
Kick it towards the direction you wish; God's path, maybe;
Lucifer's path, maybe;
Maybe, the decision should remain stationary.
A smart approach; do not force it;
Free you are to decide to follow God;
Free you are to decide to reject him.
For eternal life or eternal condemnation,
What is the choice?
Now, the decision is choice centered.
First in humbleness, you pray,
Wise is it to seek God's wisdom;
Then to others advice, carefully evaluate.
Your options, you patiently analyze;
The positive or negative you extract;
With knowledge of what God's wants,
You follow through his plan.
Beforehand of your decisions,
Great is it if implementation is with turtle steps;
As acting with caution adhere to the right thing.
Lucifer's weapon: money,
Let not money influence the way to make right decisions.
Priceless, valuable than any value of money it is,
For the favor is the choice of the Almighty God.
For at hands reach, wait on the power of the Holy Spirit;
For your path will he align with the right way.

For freewill it is;
For in the human's mind it is embedded;
Let us question ourselves and question others?
Let us grasp what is right and execute it?
Two handles it is in most things:
By one of which it ought to be,
By one of which it is contrary;

By one of which it is median;
Important may be the issues;
Baffling can the dilemma be;
Your decision, make not in rush;
For when basic principle is utilized,
Sound decision is generated:
The facts, know before responding;
To evaluate new ideas, stay flexible;
On parties involved, your eyes you open;
Before judging others,
Carefully analyze and evaluate.
Difficult may be the circumstance,
But, with knowledge and ability as embossed,
Wise should the decision be.
In sensitive issues, I ask the questions:
Am I motivated by the desire of a Samaritan?
Am I thinking godlike?
Am I unselfish? or
Am I self-centered?
Will my decision be detrimental to others?
Is it a beneficial course of action?
Will my decision be God centered?
Will my decision be man centered?
These questions, aspects they are to
Generate sound decisions.

For freewill it is;
For by instincts it is manifested,
For unconsciously mysterious factors are;
To generate, the great decisions of human life
With outcome that is reasonably acceptable.
Indeterminably, with each in their own cabin,
In their own lifestyle,
In their own life form;
Supersede not by one another.
Which bridge to cross?
How to cross it?
Which one to avoid?
Which one to incinerate?
Difficulty sets itself into action when the harvest arrives.
As considered, hardest thing to learn in life and in
Making decision it is.

Carefully you act in deciding to make change;
Not out of anger,
Not out of envy,
But first evaluate and patiently wait,
Then the decision is made.
By action of the culprit impulsive
Decision-making, severe complications set for manifestation:
Being lazy, being careless, cannot think clearly;
All give birth to poor decisions.
Not on Emotions of the moments but, your decision
You base on extreme care, a must it is
When the bridge is being burnt, to be a participant.
Decision once made, generates change;
For turning the clock back is hard;
For the past, manifestation of experience it is;
Use it as a corrector of future variables.

For freewill it is;
For it is nature of life, series
Of choices are rendered.
As life, the best choice you choose;
The feeling of others, you ignore.
Fly away on the wrong road
Mankind's direction is embedded;
A long distance it is from God's path;
As bestowed, man on the driver's seat;
God is stationed on the passenger's seat.
Such path, flowing into darkness it is.
Painful it is with such erroneous choice.
Do you realize that a mistake is made?
Are you ready to accept responsibility?
With the expressed anxiety for correction,
A teaching tool becomes the experience.
It helps, we learn, and we grow; and
Carefully the next time around,
Better choices are made.
Unpleasant may the consequences be;
But with courage and integrity as your armor,
From the right decisions, manifested reaction
Maybe social rejection, public ridicule, peer
Pressure, career derailment, or hostile persecution.
The golden word of victory is Steadfastness.
With the right decisions, solid as a rock you stay.

Co-existing with change is decision.
For any decision made, change is generated.
Once in existence, turning back is not an option.
For what is right, upright you stand.
Be on God's side, all will be well
As Higher power occupies the driver's seat.

BRING FORTH WOMEN

AFFILIATED QUOTE:

"God created man and woman in his image. There is no superior sex. There is no inferior sex. Both are created to have authority and control over all creatures. Women are special because they give life to the world. They have great wisdom, skills and compassion. Special is my mother to me. I need her to open my eyes to the world. She is an angel and the food to prosperity. Comfort I receive when I am sad. For with courage, love, and joy she fills my glass everyday".

Bring Forth Women

Bring forth women.
Progress it is to bring forth strong women.
For part of nature it is; not an accident,
But a necessity;
Dark ages it is as men ruled;
There's no voice for women,
As second class they are ranked.
Fighting for changes;
Sowing a character;
Bring back Susan B. Anthony,
And reap a destiny.
For leadership, courage, perseverance,
Hope is her attributes.
Love overshadows fear to challenge
A gender suppression system, lingered supreme.
The problem has a name;
Simply that is the fact,
It is male chauvinistic society.
From making any contribution to
Policies and progress, concealed they are.

Bring forth determined women.
Progress it is to bring forth women of thoughts
Forthrightness, sincerity, and loyalty they eye.
For it is not extraordinary;
But, core need it is.
Women of reality engulfed with strength.
Sow an act;
Bring back Rosa Parks,
And reap an act of determination.
Women willing to sacrifice themselves,
For liberty and justice, no matter what,
A change seeker she is.
For unselfishness, courage, and bravery;
It is to challenge the lion of racism.
The problem is entitled,
The fact is simply that, through
Male chauvinistic society,
Racism and ignorance lingered
For unnecessary discrimination and racism flourished.
With one race concealed from policies and progress.

Bring forth charismatic women.
Progress it is to bring forth innovative women;
For part of life it is, not a coincident.
Women of vision,
Women that is capable and independent.
Not it is extra-terrestrial;
But, significant it is as perceived.
Sow a blue print;
Bring back Oprah Winfrey,
And the success of hard work, will be reaped.
A model she is;
Even in suppressed atmosphere,
Thriving women they are;
The name is of household;
An association it is.
The problem is embossed with an emblem;
The fact is simply that
Women are suppressed in male dominated society.
Enlightenment training is necessary
To purge away contaminated minds.

Bring forth all the women.
A society that brings forth all the women,
A thriving society it is.
For women grasp to the standard of
Advancement, ability, emotion, love,
Courage, and compassion.
Societal changer they are.
For desolate and unfrequented women,
As soon as the bridge opens
With a new pathway,
To the stars they will shoot.
Just to continue the fight over and over again.
An uneasy sense of battle won;
Ongoing it is;
For such battles should have been won.
A society of many faces,
Locked in a battle;
The fact is simply that
The battle is of senseless overture;
For the call is for strong women for an overhaul.

FOREVER IT GROWS
AFFILIATED QUOTE:

"We are united and forever we'll stay. The feeling that is inside of you, no wealth can purchase it; no one can understand it; only the Almighty God knows the gravity of such love. We feel each other even when we are apart. A relationship it is, made by Divine's craftsmanship".

Forever it grows

With Divine action, together we unite,
Together we stay;
Born is our love, with the pleasure of
At each other we look.
It is fed with the necessity of seeing each other.
Impossibility of separation,
It is conducted.
With love, there is question left unanswered; for
With love, we know where, why, and when.
With love, we are compelled adhesively together;
With love, we weep with joyful tears;
With love, we hold each other in our hearts;
With love, each other is felt even if apart;
That love keeps each other in within.

Innovative is the feeling.
Inside of each of us is the feeling;
Not available for sale is the sign;
No wealth can purchase it;
No one can understand it;
Only the Almighty God can weigh the gravity of such love.
Never dissipate is that love.
Truthfulness, trustworthy, and fidelity is that love.
By a class itself is that love.
There is no other existing.
When apart, we feel each other;
When we are together, we feel each other.
The relationship is of special order.
A relationship made by Divine craftsmanship.

To faults, blind is our love;
To blames, blind is our special love;
To disagreements, blind is our relationship.
For in joy, it is inclined;
To comfort, it rest;
To ecstasy, it is excited.
Silently invisibly become my love for thee;
For I never seek to tell thee of that love;
For that love that never told can be;

For gently the wind does move it to thy sphere.
Now, my love I divulge;
I reveal my love to thee.
For now the only particles expel are
Joyful dripping tears with star-like drops.

The unexplained phenomenon saturates me.
May the love that surrounds us remain nourish;
May your love be beautiful before me?
May your love be beautiful within me?
May your love be beautiful below me?
May your love be beautiful above me?
May your love be of bounteous gift to me?
May your love be of warmth comfort to me?
May your love be bounteous all around me?
May your love be of bounteous aptitude to me?
With kindness and joy,
With trust and hope,
With fidelity into eternity,
Forever it grows.

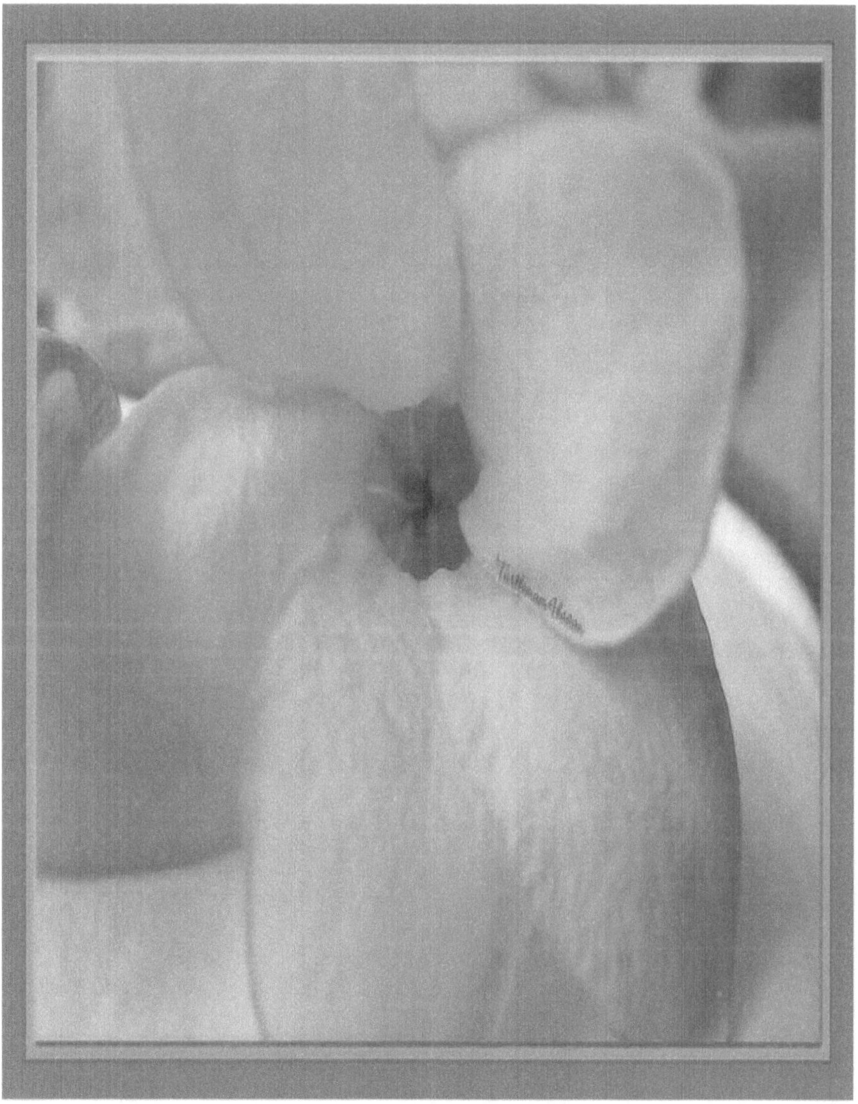

BRING ME CHILDREN

<u>**AFFILIATED QUOTE:**</u>

"My children bring joy to my heart. With them, I am determined to be better every day. A gift of blessing they are to me. I exercise my authority with caution and grace to teach them about society and life's experiences. I am responsible to help shape their future. Most significantly, I teach them about obedience to and faith in the Almighty God".

Bring me Children

Bring me children;
Leaders they can be;
Heroes they can be;
Villain they can be;
Of children in the foliage,
Quickly they spread around.
Born to be raised,
Controlled by parents;
To be trained and directed;
To be consoled and shielded;
To be overhauled by parents;
In all aspects of life to see God,
They are taught diligently.
Oh vulnerable children, sometimes
Abused, molested, and misused;
Even die with reasoning but to err.
Bring me children;
Shower them with respectful, helpful, and obedient role.
Energetic, they just want to have fun.
Hanging out with peers;
With ideas they contribute.
Whether they think too little or too much;
With chaos of thought and passion,
All confused, all amused,
Of little consideration, they acclaim.
Bring me loving children
The empty vase is filled in the domicile.

Bring me children;
A gift of blessing from God they are;
Bring me proud children;
For pride they are to parents
Who molds their values.
Bring me tailored children;
For discipline they possess.
Shape of the world's future they execute.
Bring me children;
Not arrogant, not selfish;
But in God's path they march.

Bring me charismatic children;
For tomorrow they are:
The presidents, judges, medical professionals,
Religious personnel, law enforcement
Personnel; tailor them,
Tailor them with appropriate ingredients.
Bring me respectable children;
From above, blessing is bestowed upon them.
Children, adhere to advice;
For success awaits them.
Bring me children with mirrors;
For with them comes time machines,
Gifts to their parents,
Eyeing all over again themselves.
Bring me children;
For joy they are to the family.

BRING ME MEN

<u>AFFILIATED QUOTE:</u>

"We need the best of gentlemen that are soft, meek, patient, humble, obedient, respectful, honorable, and mature. For the home, country, religion, they shape".

Bring me Men

Bring me men, free men, fresh men, forthright men
Extracted from multi-facet class; bring me devout
Men with positive attribute that is appropriate.
Bring me those dedicated men, for their children,
Living an important role as models;
Bring me men, who make the family well-being primary;
Willing to sacrifice everything for them;
Bring me men with oneness,
Who care for the family as themselves;
Bring me considerate men with respect;
Who exercise leadership role with love;
Bring me those men who maintain good family relationship.
Sensitive to their needs,
Relate to them with consideration, insight, and courtesy;
Bring me real men; men with pride;
Men with dignity, homely men;
Not absentee fathers.
Bring me men that make a difference in life.

Bring me men with a mark in the society;
For heroes they are marching to war;
They stand for what they believe in;
For their country, home and God men who strike.
Men, who trample self beneath, while others stay uplifted;
Tender but bravery they hold
In pure honor as the highest inspiration, hope manifested.
In light, they lead to victory.
For great are these men;
Lives of great men leave footprints of inspiring awe,
That makes our lives sublime.
Great is the glory of men as you
Eye the greatness of powerful nations.
Remember, the greatness was won by men with
Courage, endurance, patriotism and sense of awareness;
Honor and knowledge of purpose is in the consciousness.

Bring me men; men that are products, expressions, and reflection;
Men that shape the world, for heroes they are.
Bring me thoughtful men of loyal breeding;

Selfish not, self-centered not, arrogant not;
But, men encompassed with humility.
Bring me strong men, the secured and inspired.
Bring me the men to form an umbrella above the family;

Bring me men to form a fence around the family.
Against adversaries, they are the shield and armor.
Bring me reciprocal men, for they adopt mutual,
Selfless, confiding relationship with their spouse.
Bring me the best of gentlemen that are
Soft, meek, patient, and with calm spirit.
Bring me men who embraced the standards of their fathers;
Those who stand for God and the family.
The men of honor, the men with charisma;
Shiver not they are but, solid as a rock they remain.
Bring me valiant men that laugh and weep.
Bring me men that sow and reap by their own reputation;
These men forever stay in our hearts.

MISTAKES

<u>**AFFILIATED QUOTE:**</u>

"Everyone makes mistakes. When we make a mistake,
we must admit it and try to correct it;
So that it will not recur. As a religious person, when I make a
mistake, I pray about it and ask God for direction. Never let a
mistake become a problem; take control of it".

Mistakes

Oh world, you choose with no consideration,
Not the better part; but, with thy inward vision,
Closes the eyes; for in darkness,
Not in wisdom to believe thy heart;
But, with ignorance, the wrong choice you made.
For whether to forgive or to look better in yourself,
It is a mistake to close the eyes; accept the error,
Re-evaluate the situation.
The error, though unintentional,
Not in accordance with the facts,
Not according to your character;
Not even, in accordance with your belief.
What was your state of mind?
Now more and more you are in distress mood;
You fall,
As negative energy surrounds
You and hell reigns over your consciousness.
In that mindset, suddenly, the wrong person you are;
Self-respect is lost; intuition,
The contrary road is lost and free-dancing become the mistakes.
Don't just sit there mesmerizing about mistakes;
Drop the fear; make small decisions;
Make great decisions;
May be, proven wrong sometimes;
Those mistakes, learning tools they become.
Be religiously inclined;
Walk horizontally with your spirit;
Follow what you think God wants for you;
And inside of you,
The stumbling block you eliminate.
With new preventive measures,
Enlighten you'll be from your mistakes;
Acceptable and manageable they flow.

Oh world, for a discovery,
A metaphor of proof is the folly of errors in a paradox;
For chasing part of human dilemma,
The truth in tumultuous outburst,
Has become and additional mistakes it generates.
Let reasoning become your counselor;

And let the spirit within you rules your mind.
Mighty becomes the force of your feeling;
Now, encourage yourself;
Honestly, look at yourself.
Think not mistakes as crisis;
Think not being ashamed;
Think not perfect you must be;
Think not hiding your mistakes.
Portray not that making mistakes label you bad.
Grasp normality into thee;
Put yourself together;
Confess the mistakes;
Admit the mistakes to God;
Admit the mistakes to yourself;
Admit the mistakes to others;
Then with openness, listen to the mistakes;
Analyze the mistakes; and learn from them.
Apply corrective measures, apply adjustments.
Grow with them and wholesome
You'll become for tons of load is off your shoulder.
Mistakes, oh mistakes easy is it for you to hook your victim;
You surround everyone;
Learning tool you become as being the good teacher;
From your mistakes, enlighten you'll become;
Strengthen you'll become;
Careful you'll become;
And corrective they will be to you.

Oh world, why shower in pain and trouble?
Why avoiding religious lifestyle?
Why sitting with a closed-mind refusing to accept wrongdoing?
Why refusing to grab the mistakes?
Higher Power is waiting for your submission.
Stretch out for him.
For mankind,
Higher Power seeks stress free overshadowed environment.
For recurring mistakes, turn to Higher Power.
Admit the mistakes; seek forgiveness and reconciliation.
Then, the video will be shown.
To you, mistakes seem appropriate while ongoing;
So harder it is to recognize garbage plans.
The clock, turn back at the mistakes;

The mistakes you re-evaluate.
Then, discovered will be the attached foolishness.
As the mistakes are exposed,
The foolish ideas, you eliminate;
The foolish thoughts, you eliminate;
The foolish motives, you eliminate.
Then, active become the activation process.
You sit at ease perceiving the mistakes as normal life event.
Face them.
Correct them.
With pride abandoned,
Shame will be washed away; then, the stain dissipates.
During the span of time, for lessons learned;
For thoughts about God;
For adjustment made; document everything.
For valuable aid, it is in categorized growth.
With records, references of progress are maintained,
Repeating the past mistakes will be avoided;
No more problems will mistakes be.

ATTITUDES

AFFILIATED QUOTE:

"My attitude tells who I am. It is an aspect of my personality.
My outward attitude projects my inward attitude, revealing my
real self. As a spiritualist, my religious appetite leads me
to walk horizontally in God's path.
Therefore, being close to God in prayer, I speak to him honestly
about my feelings. By so doing, I am able to deal constructively
with my feelings. I always remember to treat others as
I will want them treat me".

Attitudes

It is a new name; a new name it is for our thoughts;
Is it the stream of consciousness?
Is it the stream of thought?
What is in the mind?
Can it be exhibited?
For it is by metaphor that this stream by nature is described.
The pace by which the stream of consciousness differs,
Is what appeals to human being.
The manner by which it is introduced;
The manner by which outward behavior
Directly projects from the inward attitude.
Born into the world it is;
Good it can be;
Bad it can be, all at the same time.
From inside, the invisible twist exposes the real self.
With triumphant feeling, planted is confidence in interacting,
Pleasant atmosphere is generated.
Not in silence, but with uncontrollable reflexes,
Deepest feeling is demonstrated;
Extemporaneously, the real self is tongue by the inside voice.
As manifested upon, particular mental or moral
Attitude sprung out as the identifying road
The human being's character;
Some of which are the consoling music;
Some of which thy barred cloud bloom;
All, within they stay as the framework of God's standards;
Thy eyes open to God's power to help,
And lead and guide by his promise.

It is in the wallpaper; things are in the wallpaper;
Unknown to all but to thee at will.
A dim shape, a shady shape, a brilliant shape,
A feeble shape, an anger shape, an arrogant shape;
Conceal behind that outside pattern.
Cough; expose each with thy tongue;
Clearer each shape gets exposed.
Though invisible, but visible it becomes
As it exposes the face behind the mask.
As negative attitude toward God erodes thy faith,

Greater trouble comes to light.
As thy faith fades, rebellion toward God increases;
The thoughts of giving up increases;
Against God you turn.
Through attitudes, personality is designed.
The occurrence of incidents, you do not choose;
But, the responsive attitude to each incident is at thy fingers tip.
As happy as the heart shall be,
So the thoughts of a healthy mind with true,
Pure and lovely thoughts exist.
Now with right attitude, so toward God is the right attitude.
Be obedient, and live effectively;
It is engulfed with respect and humility.
Abandoning hate and respect thy enemies, takes a lot of courage;
With right attitude, let the words from thy mouth picture words
From thy heart;
Let thy deed characterized you as servant of God.

It is paradoxical to landscape, that of which surrounds thee;
Thou live it in thyself;
The summit of the mountains with consoling feelings;
Patient, kind, calm attitudes;
But, with stressful feelings, the activities of with thee:
Frenzy, anguish, anger, bitterness, and selfishness.
In common, it is embossed the stream of subjective life.
The manner by which the inward and
Outward attitudes are expressed;
With two stain glasses they are:
One negative, the other negative;
One positive, the other positive;
"Birds of the same feathers"
Over and over again, Interact with each other.
Because of thy pride,
For no reasons thou lashes out at others;
Be careful, eye what is the framework of God;
Grab the stain glasses;
Apply the positive one;
Use emotion, use compassion with thy outward attitude.
Again, feel deeply and intensely inside;
Be humanly conscious with love for others.
Manifested are changes in thee.
The outward attitude portrays rejuvenated real self.

The real feeling,
Now with love, concern, compassion, and well-being;
Engulf the real person with the right countenance.

It is by faith that a new perspective is born.
That faith has a new name,
The thought of consciousness of the stream of divinity.
For it is by the stream of divinity mankind's character is embossed.
With such, assimilating God's expectation,
Fashioned is mankind's attitude.
As religiously incline we are,
Blind we become of God's power in tough times,
As a sign of positive outcomes are lost.
In fear of eternal consequences, to reconcile we move.
Inconsistency exists as lifestyle
Change is a must to walk in God's path.
When we walk with God,
Inward and outward attitudes are of concerns.
Maintaining the right character, concerned we are;
About others' feeling, concerned we are;
About extending love to all, concerned we are.
So to honor God's expectation,
Our actions and attitudes must match God's expectation;
And in God's path, horizontally we march.
With right attitudes, worldliness is insignificant;
Material goods, insignificant;
With prayer, positive attitude is bestowed upon us.
So let our identity becomes our personality;
Our feeling, character, and all aspects of attitudes;
When planted in God's garden,
Fruitful will the harvest of adjusted right attitudes be.

DIVINE GUIDANCE

<u>AFFILIATED QUOTE:</u>

"It is plain and simple, God's path for guidance is a must for any spiritualist. I follow the unquenchable light that guides me into righteousness. I focus on God. I obey; I do not give up with setbacks; I view them as temporary setbacks. I wait and seek a clear message from God. So I keep trusting God to go where he leads me, and do what he wants. With God's guidance, all my resources will be provided at the right moment".

Divine Guidance

For in the times of the pharaoh's yet,
Led by unknown wondrous power;
Hand in hand, fated are they to stroll through,
Eye the tears unseen and unknown surging immensity of life.
Not natural phenomena, but a vehicle;
The vehicle of God's presence;
Visible it is of his action and his guidance.
Of those days of old, God's pillar of cloud by day,
Pillar of fire by night;
So moved the Israelites in accordance with the
Cloud and fire as the moving matter.
According to his perspectives, God leads and guides.
The astray, he shows the proper path;
The humble and obedient, in the right path he teaches and leads;
The lost and forgotten, with unfailing love and faithfulness he leads;
All the core of Divine guidance they are.
Method of guidance it is as with specific purpose, God exercise.
In hitching a ride along God's path,
With his principles, we tag along;
Not with our own invention, but, with God's way;
Not on the shortest path, but, on the custom path of righteousness.
Willingly you follow him;
Willingly you trust him;
Willingly you obey him;
Safe path around unseen obstacles they generate.
For the end from the beginning of the adventure,
Controlled it is in God's domain.

For in the times of technology, yet,
Led by known ultimate source of power of which
Life immensity depends on it as our pathway.
Our pathway is straight, no curves, no detours;
Straight it leads to divine outreach store;
Where construction, rehabilitation are reserved.
To reach the Port of Paradise, we must sail;
Sail sometimes we must with the wind,
The wind of God.
But in physical mentality, sail we do against the wind,
The wind of mankind; drifting we are but, anchor not.

But, with the wind of God, anchor we do,
Drift not we are.
For specific purpose,
Custom-made method of the guidance, God utilizes.
Go where he leads, trust him for courage and endurance;
Trust him for confidence;
Depend on him at the right moment;
For where he takes you, he has been;
And what he gives you, he created.
Wait not for calamities to visit you, eye God now.
Open thy eyes and mind to his direction now;
For all it is positive with no negative outcome.
Of all chances, guidance which cannot be seen,
But truly clear, wherever is, is what is
Right and God on the driver seat with GPS,
Leading and directing the way to righteousness.

IF I HAD KNOWN

<u>AFFILIATED QUOTE:</u>

"If I had known, born with two relatives: maybe or maybe not; all work together with both positive and negative consequences. If I had known generates anxiety, it generates curiosity, it generates awareness, and it also generates results. Every human has an "if I had known" one time in their life. So accept the words: If I had known".

If I Had Known

If I had known that Divine guidance brings confidence,
I would have turned to God earlier.
If I had known that God systematically plans with precise target,
I would have walked his path earlier.
If I had known with inner insight the meaning of thy heart and mind,
I would have known the animus nature of earth's inhabitants.
If I had known that life is engulfed many unexpected hidden woes,
I would have planned and prepared for extraordinary events.
If I had known that sweet enticing words abode the mind
With seducing aroma mesmerizing the subject,
I would have strewed roses over my
Tongue with honey dipping words.
For when all is decoded, with no doubt there is no strife,
With better understanding as clearer vision is realized.
Then, proclaim will I that truly God knows best.

If I had known that when human being hands exposed
To the deepest cold, would freeze,
I would have been near the equator.
If I had known that the eyes movements reveal hidden agenda,
I would have exercised caution in expressing myself.
If I had known that humans' cells degrade as they get older,
I would have taken herbs to rejuvenate myself.
If I had known that worldliness is both internal and external,
I would have curtail my craving for physical pleasure and
Reduce pride in my achievements and possessions.
For now I know I have to deepen my insight,
Broaden my appreciation for unknown revelation;
I would have allow myself in in humble submission,
To mature spiritually and secularly with openness;
Then, my intuition will be used to expose new adventures.

If I had known what I am and know not what
I May be and what awaits me; then,
I will proceed with the designed journey;
For a follower I am; one that moves with divine guidance.
The journey of trust, the journey of faith
The journey of righteousness; the journey of rejuvenation;
The journey of regeneration; the journey of adaptation and success.
For only the Divine One can end it according to his perspective.

For by assigned destiny, set purpose is achieved.
For now, I know there is pleasure that comes from within;
There are raptures in the lonely shores;
There are places with no intrusion,
For the deep ocean where none venture;
There are societies of slavery, racism, and discrimination;
With technical strategies and suppression of minorities all is done.
For the sake of self-contentment, they are executed.

If I had known that in deep anguish and bitterness,
Honestly I should speak to God about my condition,
I would have expressed my feeling to God earlier,
And constructively handle the situation.
If I had known that life produces painful circumstances without introduction,
I would have conditioned myself for any contingencies,
Mentally, morally and physically.
If I had known that "in God we trust", with liberty
And justice for all is under a mask with hard cover;
The inside, oh the inside with anti-God campaigns;
Non-liberty, injustice for specific groups,
Then, I would have abode on Planet Mars.
For spiritual growth and trust in God is the answer;
Through patience, content will I be as the end point is reached.
For God's plan like lilies, pure and white will be manifested.

TAKE CONTROL

AFFILIATED QUOTE:

"Do you think you are in control? Be careful; use caution. Do not let the authority vested in you gets to your head. Refrain from manipulating others for your self-interest. Walk in God's path when you are in charge. When you are control, trust God's guidance for appropriate and reasonable action".

Take Control

Take control, move with authority amid the encircling gloom;
Control, move me onward;
For the world is of obstacles, chaotic is the surrounding;
With frenzy and confusion,
Lost I am; control, move me onward;
Hold me closer to thee, for I am lost, keep me stable;
Ask not why, take control;
Just a swift action, move me onward;
For you pace around from zone to zone;
Though through boundless hemisphere,
Not confident as I am, thou take control,
With the right steps, onward I advance.
Push not to be great, for grabbing control it is;
For many calamities await thee for pushing to control.
Use thy imagination; use the best path, trust;
By trusting, control is surrendered, you let go;
So trust becomes the way of life for control.
Thy enemies love them; by such control you transfer to God;
Then, God in control;
Giving up self-will it means, as unwanted situation be avoided.
Competently, God takes control.

Look at that, power he wants to utilize to gain control.
Caution, lust of power, not in strength;
But, rooted in weakness;
Faith is the best agent; in a package of happiness, it comes;
In the package of easier life, it comes.
Control through faith you surrender to God.
With God's guidance, all things are attached and handled.
Like a candle and a mirror, control it is;
God, the candle; mankind's heart, the mirror.
As flamed the candle, so reflect the glow in the mirror.
Glowing thy heart, that mirror;
The glow, that glow of God shines in it.
So in the mirror thou stay as God controls thee.
You tried power; now you want to use the weapon, love;
Trying you are to get others to love you.
No, no, no human can try to by ordering others to love.
Beware, control is like a drug, powerful with encompassed,

Disappointments and troubles.
As you realized, on thou way always, things go not;
With selfless countenance, you take control.

Roll on; thou slick but in dark deep ocean waves;
Expecting to get over, but get caught in thy track.
Watch out, drown you may;
The control may stop with the shore.
Your way always things go not,
For if stays in silence, learn from thy visitation;
Aggravation is limited; the thirst to take control shrinks.
Manipulate others not for thy own benefit when in control;
Choose who and what will control you;
Choose who and what you will control.
On God's path should your choice be base.
With this, follower of the Higher Power thou become.
Space-out become self-centeredness and self-control;
Part of thee become thought control as
The mantle is passed over to God's control.
Plain and simple it is; God owns the world, knows the future.
Though out of control is the world, in place is God,
In control is God;
Unshakeable he stays with the world's problem;
With his attributes, he takes control.

A NEW PATH

AFFILIATED QUOTE:

"New surroundings, new situations may frighten you; but, faith in God will counter any fear and strengthen you to venture a new path".

A New Path

What a new path it is? I woke up and there it is.
Do I know what I want? Do I know I want to do?
It is simple, follow the mind communicator.
I grab myself together to eye all the possibilities
Of all, there is only one. The one, is the
Path of God. That path is the new path.
It is of moral issues; it is of mental issues;
It is of spiritual issues; it is of physical issues;
The new path, nourished with discernment it is.
The old ways abandon, the new ways embrace.
Differently, you start seeing things. To a new world,
You are open. Obedient you become;
Humble you become; submissive you become;
Faithful you become; and on God Almighty
You become dependent.
Rearrange will your attitude be.
Your desires and motives become rejuvenated.
Spring-up in you is a new life.
All is done for a better pathway, a new path.

The road ahead, do you know?
Oh look, they are returning; ask those coming back.
Down to a new road you sway;
Change in your life you seek; familiar not is that road.
The old path only you know.
For change is frightening.
Take the step to a new path; excited you should be.
Be attentive; follow the track, the map;
The trip, enjoyable it will be.
That map, the map of God's guidance; forever it stays.
Picture not the distance, for matter not it is;
For the first step, that step though difficult, venture you should.
If the spirit within you withers,
So too will the world built around you.
Spirituality breathes life into us.
God's spirits breathe life into us.
We start to feel enhanced; we start to feel hope within.
So all over again,
Gradually being rebuilt is our entire world.

Where are the situations?
Existing are the situations.
New situations, new surroundings, new path
Frighten they can be.
Okay it is to experience fear;
Paradoxically, okay not it is, normal not by fear,
It is to be paralyzed.
For an indication of doubt it generates.
Doubt not God, for unimaginable
To guide is God's ability. Through faith in him,
Through faith in him, unlimited is his ability to take care of us.
With hyssop, he cleanses us, generating a new birth,
A new path, fine-tuning our attitudes from inside out.
With God not satirical; but, ever new, ever moral,
Ever spiritual; he delights, instructs, and direct the obedience;
You may sigh with the many of new things,
Wail fully recount the old woes; but with the journey,
Open is the sky with delightful dazzling stars.
Though bumpy is the road and expectation;
With God's guidance, smoothly becomes the new path.

PROBLEMS

<u>AFFILIATED QUOTE:</u>

"In the word of God, involved is the unity of humanity calmness and the wholeness of human problems. Everyone will someday experience problem. How you handle it, ' is the key to expanding or reducing the problem. As religious as I am, when I am experiencing trials and troubles, I first visit my counselor, God Almighty, and spill out my mind to him. Then, patiently I wait for his guidance. After experiencing problems, you may become stronger with endurance to handle situations and deepen will become your character.
Stay faithful to God; no matter how impossible the problem seems to you, God has a solution for it. Pray, pray and wait patiently for God".

Problems

There are loud wailings, sighs, and lamentations
Sounding through the moonless air;
Strange tongue and horrible language have become my speech
As I weep with words of pain.
My anger increases, my voice becomes louder;
In tumult I am, as the whirling wind dominates the atmosphere.
In darkness, I struggle seeking an end to this dark hole.
When darkness falls, attached with troubles and difficulties,
Encouraged happiness should be our countenance;
For our patience and character will be developed through;
Trusting God to act on our behalf,
An opportunity to honor God in our present situation,
From God's perspective for us, we wait.
Easy it is to focus on our weaknesses; excluded, is Higher Power;
Just by simply including a Higher Power to do something,
Well done will be the outcome;
In boosting the weak areas, God provides strength, courage, and ability.
Walk, you must rough road;
Climb, you must high mountains;
Disagreements, you must encounter;
Arguments, you must experience;
Battle, you must fight;
Problems, you must solve;
Adjustments, you must make; all for the sake of growing.
For bestowing strength upon us to meet challenges, God promises;
Paradoxically, to eliminate challenges, God promises not.
To God you always turn for problems.

Complain not about your struggles,
As opportunity for growth, accept them.
In rough times, thank God for walking the road with you;
For help, ask him to grant you courage
And endurance to keep on going;
For maturity under hardship, appreciate God more;
As good as God is,
Your problems he handles side by side with you.
Defeated you feel,
When burden and misfortune pay you a visit;
Welcome them with pleasure for fertilizer

They are to your attributes;
As stronger and develop they become.
Eye upward and forward, not inward with problems;
As stronger becomes thy character,
So arriving are opportunities to comfort others experiencing problems.
Stand you take on God's path with troubles and tribulations.
For the award of worthiness of God's Kingdom,
Through such experience we achieve.
Significantly to the religiously acclaimed,
Doing good and being obedient sometimes may bring suffering;
Humble submission sometimes may bring hardship;
Suffering sometimes may continue or even get worse;
Life sometimes may become unpleasant and miserable;
When all are manifested, assume not that
God's favor is distance away.
For God is silently molding your world.

Oh lack of faith, the sweetener for generating series of problems;
Stop taking over for God.
With effort out of line with specific direction,
Retract; wait a little while for God to act.
Out of frustration and accusation, you strike out and
Want someone else to admit the error and seek forgiveness.
No more; enough is enough;
Seek God's guidance now;
For with humble submission, your problem he will solve for thee.
Run away not from thy problems;
Evaluate to find the cause of the problems;
Work to find a solution to thy attitude.
In spite of how complicated, how messy the situation is,
God possesses the ability to change the problem to good.
By careful thought, problems can be solved;
By re-arranging thy priorities, problems can be solved;
By counseling and good advice, problems can be solved;
By prayers only, problems can be solved.
Solve thy problems in whatever way you choose;
But, with prayer, determined you must be to quiet thy thought,
Emotion, listening, and complain not.
With great problems, to exercise his omnipotence,
Placed we are in perfect position to grant God the opportunity.
Fear, the culprit producer of wrong assumption sometimes,
Lead to lies and instigator for more problems.
Make no assumption,

Try to grasp complete understanding of circumstances;
On the intervention of God, wait.

Drifting more and more into the hole makes life tougher;
Disappointment is adhered into the picture.
Ride the storm with God;
Though painful and inevitable are problems and difficulties,
Eye as growth opportunity and prevail with God.
Talk to God; open up to him; establish a relationship with him.
The number of hair on thy head, God knows;
Greatly concern and interested in thy welfare is God.
When the decision becomes too heavy for thee,
God is on thy side carrying it with thee.
Never lost sight on God; never encourage negative attitude;
The possibilities, you weigh carefully and with God's might,
The problem will be solved.
Facing towering problems complain not;
Act; jump not to choose the lesser of two evils;
Evaluate the right one first; change, do what is required.
Be strong with confidence to fight effectively by trusting God.
Know God; know God's history, his curriculum vitae;
Be courageous, fight effectively more;
By God's might, you'll be upheld.
Thy relationship with God is of extreme significance,
Just like life is more than material good.
The gift of power to overcome obstacles is handed over to humans by God;
Fear and skepticism, the negative energies,
Activate the door of difficulties dominating our lives.
Only through courage, endurance, trust, and faith
Will insurmountable obstacles be diminished.
Sinful act or unwise choice resurrects the destroyer, problems.
Your sin, confess; the behavior, change;
During the storm, petition God to strengthen you.
To handle problems,
Change not scenery;
Change not location;
Change not job; the source of the problems, face;
The existence of the problems, eye as normal;
The magnitude of the problems, exaggerate not;
Unto thyself and thy problems, look not;
Unto God, you reach-out.
With the right attitudes and God's guidance, the problems will be solved.
Just as fire purifies silver in the melting process,

So refined become thy character as problems
Generate new and deeper wisdom with the key to discern the truth.
Character builder problem is;
Sensitivity toward other problems, it is,
To strengthen faith and trust, it is;
For experiencing problems may be God's plan for believers.
Attached to every aspect of life is problem;
For the religiously acclaimed,
Stormy weather and calm oceans be thy gifts;
Be prepared for surely the storm will arrive;
To stress, surrender not; for resilient you must remain.
Unto God, faithful you stay;
Pray, be humble, trust, submissive, and thy journey, continue.
For God in control will take care of thee.

PROMISES

<u>AFFILIATED QUOTE:</u>

"Words from thy tongue reveal thy character. Do not expel something for the sake of expelling. Do not make a vow just to satisfy your desires. Do not make promises with evil intentions. Abide by your promises. If there is a doubt in fulfilling a promise, do not make it. With God, be careful what you promise in prayer because he takes your promises seriously. We must act like God. God is faithful; so we should be faithful in all promises made".

Promises

It is of great importance that what is said is what is meant.
Daily should words expel from thy mouth, are words of trust.
For some do not care what they say;
What makes them feel good, they just expel or
What makes the other party feels good.
There is no more trust;
There is no more fidelity;
There is no more responsibility;
There is no more confidence;
Just a word becomes the word of mankind;
The word disappears in the atmosphere.
Dedication to our promises must be emphasized;
Built we are in the image of God. If God keeps his promises,
Likewise, mankind should comply with what is promised.
Before rendering vow, essential it is to evaluate it thoroughly.
Once rendered, the vow must be honored.
The core of life is promise, as everyone makes promises.
Most broken, only few honored.
Disrespectful it is; dishonorable it is; sinful it is;
Heartbroken it is; pathetic it is; and an abomination to God
In promising something not intended.
Be trustworthy, be faithful, and be reasonable;
Hold on to what is promised.

Naturally, it is with words of thy mouth that mankind persuades
Themselves that promises will be kept.
Imbecilic is the belief, as
Embedded within the mental imbalance;
Dissipating with the period and frequency of occurrence;
To dishonored promises, it leads.
Listen with credulity and satisfy the promises;
It shows great courage to carry out promises;
Responsibility in acceptance means carrying;
Executing with determination and courage means fulfilling;
Regardless of personal sacrifice, it is carried out.
Enough it is just to say yes;
Enough it is just with thy word;
Questionable is thy sincerity.
Promises, you keep;

Promises of sin, keep not;
Rash promises, make not;
For wise and self-controlled should thy
Attitude be with justified promise.
More than what can be performed, promise not;
For according to thy capability with good intention,
Always promise.
For in good faith, honor what is promise.

Occupied with multiple tongues is your conscience.
Expel from each are several components:
Some are of villain;
Some are of virtue;
Some are of uncertainty;
Some are positive;
Some are negative.
Thou make promises; thou think noble because thou perceive noble;
Thou promise only to do thy best; so live out thy life.
Live in harmony with thy vow; live in harmony with thy true intention;
Make all that is promised, promises of truth.
Promises made, should be promises fulfill.
For God expects thee to act honorably despite encountered difficulties.
Binding as a written contract should thy words be;
In truth, thou speak;
In truth, thou live;
In thy enthusiasm make not hasty promises;
For God weighs thy commitment,
The frame of thy heart, he knows;
Step by step, should thy commitment be demonstrate.
As thou grow spiritually with God, so growth is thy knowledge of God;
So increase is thy faith;
Positive becomes thy attitude; so trustworthy becomes thy promises.

In today's world, words are just hearsay;
It is prevalent condition that mankind just open thy mouth
Just for the sake of opening it.
Like the phrase:
Hear what I say; do not what I say;
Do not what I do; for we must be people of integrity.
When we act, we must act with what the inward spirit dictates.
Most are ignorant of their inner spirit,
Adamant they are about accepting the existence of such.
In plain diction, promise what is intended.

Promise with thy capability;
Promise in faith;
Promise selflessly.
The stars, the moon, the sun all promised each other
That by the season,
Each will abide with appointed time and obligation.
Remember, thy true image is revealed by what is promised.
Once made, compliance must be followed.
A life of trust and a life of responsibility we must abide by.
No matter what thou do,
Words expel from thy mouth,
For they donate full responsibility for thee.
In all you do no matter what, promises must be kept.

LONELINESS

AFFILIATED QUOTE:

"Our consciousness and perspectives determine how we perceive life. If you think you are a loser, you will be lonesome; if you think you are abandoned, you will be lonesome; if your mind video misery within you, then loneliness will dominate your life".

Loneliness

Why are you starring looking so sad?
Why are you so lost?
Why are you so settled on your own corner?
Detrimental thoughts occupied thy mind.
Why so perceived?
Arise; shake off the disturbances from thee.
Pick up thy whole self; start moving.
The beginning just started.
Think, analyze, and evaluate situation.
God is stretching his hands toward thee.
Let him in your life.
Surrender control over to him.
For with God, comforted you'll be by the Holy Spirit.

Alienated thou feel; cut-off thou feel;
Like a parasite you are with the wind,
Loneliness is spreading all over you.
Slowly you are affected with feelings of isolation;
With the crowd, additional isolation is generated.
Go around; sincere friends, seek;
Superficial friends, seek not.
To God, you turn;
Ask him to reveal such friends to thee.
Now with the challenges, sincere friends you seek.
One who listens; one who cares;
One who offers assistance in good times or bad times.
Embraced will thou be with comfort and selfless gesture.

Religion you cling to but,
Shaky is thy faith.
Temptation, waive off;
Think not of yourself as the only remaining faithful to God's task.
For thyself, feel not sorry;
For the good thou involve in, self-pity will be diluted.
Are you feeling lonesome in standing up for God?
No o.., wake up;
In silence, God is building a worldwide Kingdom
With faithful followers, the word is being spread around.
Join the wagon;
No matter how minute is thy faith, become part of the flocks.
You will not be alone as the Holy Spirit comforts thee.

As individualistic, self-centered is the world;
Lost, is multitude with a negative perception of others;
You are not alone,
As stated by God's revelation.
For the Holy Spirit comforts thee in truth;
In knowledge, the Holy Spirit teaches thee;
In virtue, the Holy Spirit reveals the truth to thee;
In tribulation, the Holy Spirit helps thee;
With thy situation, be content;
In obedience, focus on God;
In humility, be submissive to him.
With all the executed appropriate actions,
God will address your tribulation and trouble.

Lack of faith, lack of confidence;
Now overcome you are by extreme weakness;
Sending you are, the wrong outlook of abandonment.
In so much doubt, you are hung between to act or sleep.
Chaos of thoughts occupied thy mind;
Chaos of passion occupied thy mind;
Chaos is all over;
In disarmament, your world has become.
Evil is now part of your adobe.
Solution you must sort before it is too late;
You keep sniffing around but none can be found.
Suddenly the name Higher Power resonates inwardly;
With no hesitation, unto God you surrender.

Loneliness the culprit of depression,
Consumes mankind's reasoning power;
To the lonesome, none existence is life;
In the darkness of Hades you wish to abode;
All that you eyed is negative occurrences;
Additional burden of responsibility is bestowed by society,
Increasing stress and generating isolation from others.
With a rejuvenated moral and mental attitude,
Unto God you surrender without hesitation.
With his GPS and in control,
To the appropriate destination,
God takes thee;
Carefully, loneliness is treated with the love of God.
Be ready always for changes around you;
Stay flexible and to change, you adopt.

Aware you become of the aspects of loneliness;
Willingly and able in a gradual manner,
Your attitude towards loneliness, become positive.
The pressure from defeated mind, you no longer adhere to.
In different activities, different acquaintances you are now involved; With
dedication, you are now with trusted friends.
Your religious belief has molded you into a new creature;
Now encompassed you are with humility, trust, and faith in God.
With the rearranged and established attitudes;
Loneliness is no longer an issue,
As God with his GPS, stands erect rendering you guidance.

PROGRESS

AFFILIATED QUOTE:

"Your status, you measure; your position, you measure; your condition, you measure. All in a manner of stage-to-stage process or degree-to-degree process. As you do, advancement you make; so be the core of progress".

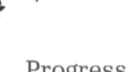

Progress

Earth, the world of many windows to thy heart;
Magnetized it is with glories and woes;
Weather it is melancholic or joyous, but it is there.
Not with voluntary control but, of consciousness of the mind.
Whether it is marching forward,
Marching stagnated or backward,
No matter how it marches, it shines forward from countless sources.
As gradually it progresses, it moves through
The windows of opportunity as truth manifest itself
By projecting how progressive thy effort has brought thee.
Part of nature it is; it is not an accident;
So are the branches of progress.
With life, to a greater, broader, and complete dimension,
Existence and progression comingle with each other.
To mankind, they are necessitated.
From want to want,
From enjoyment to enjoyment not, will life progress.
Life is its own journey as it
Progress with its own change and movement;
By culture and tradition, it presupposed mankind's perspectives.
Let thine heart eye the real picture;
To the voice of nature, listen;
To the truth, turn;
To the goodness of progress, turn;
To the present, hold;
To the past, hold not;
For clinging to the past makes you unwilling to turn away completely.
As you accommodate pieces of the past,
Progress with God will be absent.

With this fast-moving society,
Quick victories we seek;
In our lives, quick changes we seek.
Life's long progress is our journey with God
With God, easy it is to grow inpatient
As we abandon hope due to turtle steps appearance of things.
As perceived, blinded we are situated to view progress.
Look back, re-evaluate your position;
Now with eyes open,

You can see that God in silence,
Never stop working.
Drained out will you be with such present condition
As growing close to God you are kept from.
By your shortcomings,
Incomplete you feel;
Unfinished you feel;
Distressed you feel;
By those shortcomings, unprogressive in your life you feel;
Your present condition,
The joy of growing closer
To God, don't allow it not to rob you.
Seek the trusted solution,
God Almighty, who on your behalf,
Promise to cross the finish line with you.
The desire to live beyond expectation,
Is the universal innate based on progress?
Only by an individual and within the individual,
Real progress is realized.
Part of nature it is; not an accident,
As a necessity irreproachably, progress exists.

With a society of so many obstacles and uncertainties,
Mankind is not locked into failures;
By reason of thy imagination,
By reason of thy emotional subtlety and toughness;
Make it possible for thee not just to accept failures,
Nor dwell in uncertainties, but
With progress, change with it.
In stages, the process of advance is marked;
In stages, the direction of advance is marked;
The process and direction now is core.
If according to thy direction one advances,
Thy heart's desires are satisfied.
For lessons thoughts during the period are kept,
For recorded thoughts of God deeds are kept,
Spiritual growth and valuable aid they are.
With maintenance of records,
Check-up and evaluation of progress to
Prevent repeating similar mistakes can be performed.
The test of progress is based not on whether
The abundance of the conscious mind is added to,

Nor of the spiritual and moral consciousness; but
Based it is on whether enough effort is exerted for a change.
Progress is tied in with religious belief.
Dependency on God's guidance is resurrected.
With God now in control guiding us,
Even though there is flat plain to walk;
Bumpy roads to drive;
High mountains to climb;
Rough seas to sail;
Continuously, progress flourishes.

VICTORY

AFFILIATED QUOTE:

"Every human being seeks victory someway, somehow. Victory encompasses multi-facet aspects of life. You must face your struggles or issues head-on in order to become an overcomer. When you are facing a difficult situation that is beyond your control, remember that there is Higher Power to render a solution. Be grounded in God. With God, victory will come when you hold on to your ground".

Victory

In all aspects of life,
Victory is sort for spiritual, political, moral, physical,
And religious interests.
Victory for survival;
Victory in all shapes and forms;
Victory at all cost;
Victory through strength and work of God Almighty;
Victory in spite of all obstacles;
Victory in spite of fear;
Victory on bumpy roads;
Victory on long and high mountains; and
Victory on plain grounds.
Struggle and battle, we all face;
Areas of weakness, we all have;
Secret of victory, we all must find;
Situations we feel we cannot win, we all must;
Admit the futility of human effort.
Trust God to save;
Seek the power of God's Spirit;
Stay away from temptation; and
Seek support from other religious colleagues.
For God's power works effectively through those who
Depends on him and acknowledge his role in their life.
Your fear, face head-on;
Standing side by side with you through the ordeal,
Find trustworthy people along the way.
Be grounded in God; hold on to your ground;
Victory will come on commitment and obedience,
Not on strength or numbers.
So dependent is victory.

Sometimes in our lives,
An extraordinary event arrives in our abode unannounced,
Situation becomes difficult beyond our control.
Do we ask ourselves what options or
Steps are available toward a solution?
Maybe, we need only to take the first step;
The steps bring the chain of solution leading to eventual victory.
We applaud ourselves when we overcome.

Sometimes we look forward for that day of victory.
Whether it is a victory of the enemy,
Victory of sin,
Victory of struggle,
Victory of illness;
All is welcome at the peak of the mountain.
You feel good about the outcome;
You feel proud of yourself.
When you look back and realized the distance completed,
You feel more proud of yourself.
After such great victory,
Watch out as these are the times
When you are very susceptible to fall into sin;
As you feel confident;
As you feel relaxed;
As you feel ready to celebrate;
Vulnerability sets itself in your path;
Your defenses are let down during the time of excitement,
Open you become to all of types of temptations and attacks.
Be strong and hold on to your new path;
Hold on to your belief;
Victory is hand-stretch away to grab.

Complain we do about predicament
When nervous and afraid of what is ahead.
On negative aspects of a situation, we focused.
The positive ways:
Moving out with trust;
Moving out in faith toward God;
Focus on God's direction and promises;
In God's path, horizontal and parallel we march.
Quick changes in our lives we seek;
Quick victories in our struggles we seek;
Quick changes to overcome expected sin we seek;
All we seek with available limited time.
Changes may take time;
Victories may take time;
Work with God;
With God, a lifelong process it is;
Impatient we grow with God;
As we perceive things are moving too slow,
Overcome you become with feeling of giving up hope;

The process seems so difficult;
But when you look back, you realized that God is always working;
He never stopped working.
With the absence of enthusiasm,
Enough not is it to fight;
By determined spirit and morale induced in the fight,
Victory can only be won over the struggles.
Victory, the word of joy, jubilation, and celebration,
Render your heart's desire to overcome.
For with continued relationship with God,
Victory is always thine.

DOING THE RIGHT THING

<u>AFFILIATED QUOTE:</u>

"What, are you concerned about saving your image than being in horizontal path with the Almighty God? Stop that foolishness? Oh, you are worried about getting caught than doing what is right. It is a shame; awake, let your fear of getting caught be a warning to doing the right thing. Stay strong in your faith in God and do the right thing no matter the threat or consequence as long as your action is in line with God's command".

Doing the Right Thing

In doing the right and fair things you eye;
Your desires, your settlements,
All centered in the right path;
But, sinful and stubborn is our society;
Executed wrong deeds are the daily norm;
All done in disregard of what is right.
Enough is it to confess our failures;
Enough is it to live up to standards set by God;
Enough is it to implement the standards with action.
No matter what, the right thing you do;
Even with unpopular action and maybe standing alone,
The right deed you execute;
Even when the stakes are high,
The right deed you execute;
On to God's way, you steadfastly hold.
Your opponents, you perceive with respect not as problems;
Though difficult may the decision be,
The consequences and effects you view by
Standing up for what is right, and
Your direction, geared toward God's direction.
In promoting spiritual enhancement, strength, and growth,
People may scorn and ridicule you;
People may respond with mockery;
People may respond with persecution;
For friends and associates may feel disappointed;
For you may disobey authorities;
But with courage, for what is right, take a bold stand;
Walk in God's path; stand for God;
Plentiful will God rewards you.

Let us question ourselves?
Let us question those who question us?
Whatever is on the table, hear;
What point are they leading to, decipher;
Their true intention, find;
Ask yourself, is doing the right thing in their agenda?
Maybe angry;
Maybe with grudge;
Maybe fearful;

Maybe lazy;
Maybe do not want to get involved.
Knowing what is right and failed to act on it,
A fallacy it is with such action.
Negative thoughts and practices, eliminate;
Hinder will your relationship with God be for failure to act.
Content not is God if we do the right thing some of the time;
Content is God if the right thing is done all the time.
Think not that doing the something efficient or thoroughly,
Mean it is good;
Your measurement, that measure;
The measure of compliance, obedience, and righteousness
By the Rule of God's word it should abode.
Sometime fly away we become as
The distinction between right and wrong cannot be identified;
Our penetration,
Centered it is on material rewards;
For destructive is such path.
For it is only when right and wrong are distinctive,
That implementation of the right action is activated.

By the right view, the right aspiration;
The right conducts, the right effort, the right mindfulness;
The path of God is exhibited close by;
No matter what, it enables us to do the right thing,
The right way, you walk.
What is it all about? You sometimes wonder.
What else, will peers or colleagues welcome me? You ask.
What others think of you? shouldn't matter;
Not your interest.
Whatever others pressure you to do, shouldn't matter;
Not your interest.
Saving face than doing the right thing, shouldn't matter;
Not your interest.
More worried about getting caught doing the right thing,
Shouldn't matter,
Not your interest.
Embarrass to admit foolish mistakes, shouldn't happen;
Not your interest.
For fear of getting caught with dishonest position,
Is a warning sent to be embraced with the right thing.
For not looking good;
For not admitting your mistakes;

No matter what;
Doing the right thing should be your primary agenda.
No matter what position you take,
Doing the right thing, with God's path you are aligned.
Act inwardly in selfless gesture;
For God watches our every action,
Plentiful will your reward be.

CHOICES

<u>**AFFILIATED QUOTE:**</u>

"Choices, by freewill they are made. For any choice made, adhered are attachments. Whether positive or negative effect is generated, responsibility falls on the decision maker. Right choices bring positive result to a situation. Therefore, we should always make wise choice horizontally to God's command".

Choices

Trial to every mankind it is at the rise of the sun;
At the end of the day is the sunset,
The time for evaluation it is.
At the shine of the moon and the stars,
The time of reflection and passing of judgment it is.
In unity, all works in coordinated fashion,
According to thy choice made throughout the day.
As order is bestowed upon thy life,
That day, think about it.
To make choices, you must learn.
Quick route to prosperity, not;
Quick route to pleasure, not;
Quick route to make you feel that you belong, not;
On lust, extravagance, and vainglory, not;
Not just for pleasure,
Not short range pleasure,
For what, actions generate positive or negative consequences.
Capable are others of enticing thee into negative activities;
March away, maintain thy integrity;
If thy path is horizontal with the Almighty God,
Coordinated and effective will your choice be.
God renders choices; we sometimes choose wrongly;
With wrong choices, trouble maybe generated.
We learn, we grow, and consequentially,
Make better choice in the future.
With choices, there are consequences;
We accept them as they teach us to think
And choose wisely and more carefully;
Clear perspective of life and peace are generated.
By freewill we choose;
For God doesn't halt wrong or right choices;
With knowledge of God's attributes,
Centered will our choice be in God's path.

Choice is life;
Life is about choice.
Life is the accumulative total of our choices.
By freewill, one of the cores available is choice.

Choices can be physical or spiritual;
To be spiritual, thy choice should be spiritual;
To be physical, thy choice should be physical;
On honesty, obedience, faith, and humbleness
Centered they are on spiritual choices;
On integrity, honesty, and societal ethics
Centered they are on physical choices.
Grouped together they are as directional determinants.
When good choices are made,
Opportunities for good outcomes are set into motion.
When evil choices are made,
Opportunities for wrong outcomes are set into motion.
Stabilized will you be with obedience and submissiveness
For decisions made in accordance with God's command.
Decisions contrary to God's command,
Welcome the arrival of confusion and destruction.
Right choices bring light to attitudes,
The light becomes the mother of positive reflection on integrity.
Obedience brings strong safeguard with security in thy life.
Glued to choices are attachments;
Good are some attachments;
Bad are some attachments.
Positive or negative effect may be caused by decisions made.
In making decision question thyself:
Is my choice good for me and others?
Is it based on horizontal and parallel path with God's command?
Is selfishness a factor of such action?
Is the choice made for the glory of God?
Now, take a long deep breath and make the right choice.

Captive we are without choices,
For hollow will obedience exists.
With two stained glasses available, choices are available;
The obedient glass with prosperity, you can choose;
The disobedient glass encompassed with misery and sadness,
You can choose.
When stain glasses abode with thee,
The stained glass with obedience, you choose.
Live for ourselves, we can;
Live in-service to God, we can;
Our way, the dead-end street,
The way to nowhere it is.

REV JOHN

Now the in-service to God you choose,
As it is the street to prosperity and eternal life.
Sometimes available,
Are only two apparent choices, both of apparent wrong choices.
With such, lose not sight of what God wants;
To get the right choice, more choices you seek;
By so doing, the choice that honors God, we may find.
Winner we become as we strive each day for better decisions;
Winner we become with good and active choices;
As choices become active, so the old ways are abandoned.
Good we start to feel as decisions are now based on the right path.
The choice to make is always available;
To enjoy freedom, we must control ourselves;
Specific perspectives, we must have;
Good choice, we must make.
With every choice made, difference is made in our lives:
Some negative, some positive, and some neutral;
All core of happiness, sadness, stability, or chaos
The chosen choices are by your freewill;
By your choices, captive you may be held;
Free, you may be set with the appropriate choices.

SPIRITUAL RENEWEL

AFFILIATED QUOTE:

"As spring is for new growth, re-growth; likewise, spiritual renewal denotes rejuvenation, regeneration, and rebirth. As the world is a cycle, so is our life and so be spiritual renewal. Spiritual renewal is part of existence. Always remember that spiritual renewal begins and ends with the Almighty God. Walk horizontal and parallel in God's path for your renewal".

Spiritual Renewal

There is chaos, tumult is all over,
The foundation is even shaking;
Now with nowhere to hide, remember,
God is in control;
By the turn of events, his power is never diminished.
Without God's knowledge and permission,
Nothing happens.
When encompassed with the feeling of banishment and seclusion;
On to Paradise, you eye and sprint to God;
Justice and goodness, he will restore.
The engulfment of spiritual renewal arrives,
But with a package that must be satisfied;
Retain God's attributes, especially his compassion.
Despite being ridiculed, scorned, or persecuted,
Hold strong, never give up.
Keep on going, to your integrity and perseverance, glued.
From your life, denounce and aggressively remove
Evil influences through discernment.
Those who caused compromise to your faith,
Cease and desist association;
Equal yoke partners and associates, seek;
Your life, you begin to rebuild with God;
Your commitment, you renew with God;
Others, you treat as you would have them treat you;
Those who cannot repay you, help;
Intercede for people, who are feeble;
Love and peace, you extend to all.
Remain obedient, humble, submissive, selfless, and faithful
For trustworthiness, you will be refined by the Almighty God;
Now, molded, generously rest your contribution to God's purpose.

Like the season it is;
Without the harsh conditions of winter,
Spring would not be so pleasant.
Forward we look for something better;
New growth, re-growth, things become anew;
Life starts to spring up again;
So be a spiritual renewal.
After encountering great obstacles,

Trust God;
Hold strong and wait for God to deepen
Your character and strengthen your faith;
A rebirth you then experienced.
With confidence you abode with God,
Inwardly and outwardly he will rejuvenate you.
With a continuous spiritual renewal,
Your relationship with God will spring-up.
By listening, information about God you accept and absorb.
The meaning and implications of life you understand by learning;
Now into action,
You implement what you have learned and understood by obeying.
Spiritual renewal begins and ends with God,
As the truth he reveals to us, as he lives among us,
As to his truth, he enables us to respond.
With vision and sharing, spiritual renewal commenced.
The revelation, share with enthusiasm and inspiration with others.
In our mind, by his perspectives,
Through assigned task from him,
God plants ideas to accomplish his purpose.
With one person with the vision to express,
With the other to turn the vision to reality, God utilized.

Great is the cycle of ages;
As the sum of things being renewed,
Upon one another, mortal lives dependent.
Like family,
For spiritual and physical renewal of the family tree,
The touch is being passed from one generation to another.
From inwardly, commence spiritual renewal;
For if the spirit inwardly dissipates or withers,
So be the entire world around us.
So dissipate our love, attitude, spirit, relationship, perception,
Beauty; all for renewed life in us are starving.
Full of parts is our life: mind spirit, and body.
All for an equilibrium of what life needs.
Daily renewal is part of existence.
Like tree or plant, each day with the sunrise, life is bestowed upon it.
So mankind, on a daily basis,
Start over again and over and over again;
On new growth, life of mankind is dependent.
To bring new ideas and growth into our lives,
At our disposal are many ways:

New ideas, you invite to your life;
Flexibility to change, you are opened to;
Spiritual renewal from whatever formats it pays a visit,
You accept with open hands.
By so doing, your spiritual life will be made afresh;
Onward growing it will be.
You see joy;
The sunset, you start to observe;
The sunset, you start to understand and grasp;
Now clearly, will spiritual renewal be eye.

POSSESSION: THE WAY TO HANDLE THEM

AFFILIATED QUOTE:

"Material possession is a necessity in today's world. Money is part of possessions. The love of money is the means to realities of life. Avoid having a burning desire for possessions. In doing so, you will be enticed to do the wrong thing or going to the wrong places. Let your desires stay within the premises of God's purpose and command".

Possessions: The Way to Handle them.

It has changed from the days of old,
Necessity is now material possessions.
The feel of confidence, satisfaction, and complacency,
Generated are they from wealth and luxury,
At ease people live with such possessions.
Envy, greed, self-centeredness and selfishness,
Maybe the ingredients for the love of
More and more possessions.
When blessed with material possessions,
God, you thank always.
Be not proud, be not arrogant, be not self-praise;
Be Well-to-do in good works; generous, you should be;
Humble, you should be; considerate, you should be;
Sharing with others, you must be willing.
No matter how much you possess;
No matter how wealthy you are;
Everything you have is through a vital relationship with God.
In a short period of time, wealth can shrink unexpectedly;
In your life,
Demonstrate that God is the controller of your possessions;
A caretaker he is.
Only in God, true contentment can be found;
As only the Almighty God can supply all of our needs.
Covet not; envy not;
For if enticing desires move you to such feeling,
Relax, re-evaluate and pray to God
To extinguish negative desires and for guidance,
Turn to God.
For the failure to put God first in your actions,
His blessing he will withhold from you.
Put the Almighty God on the driver's seat,
Now, watch the fruitfulness and productiveness in your life.

By multitude, it is known that
Possessions do not make you happy;
Greed and materialism, you must avoid.
As manager, you consider yourself for
Possessions under your care;
As owner, you consider yourself not.

Efficiently you must take care of God's property.
Your possessions,
Share some with the needy and poor;
With the burning desire for possessions,
The arrogance from success,
Your freedom and enjoyment maybe lost.
Enticed you maybe into doing the wrong thing,
Or the wrong places, you go.
Such actions can both entice and enslave you,
If strayed away from God's desires are your motives.
Hesitate we might be to abandon
Material possessions, status, fame, and comfort;
Such hesitation is generated from false attraction.
For staying committed to God's word and purpose,
Short-run loss it may cause you;
Being steadfast, choosing God over possessions,
Stronger and stronger you stand
As one day you will acquire possessions beyond all measures.
Focus on what you have;
Focus not on what you don't have;
If you do,
Your attitude towards wealth, prestige, and comfort, examine.
Your priorities re-examine;
Your source of power set;
God's purpose and command,
Replant at your pinnacle.

The love of money as a possession,
The love of money as a means to realities of life,
Distinguish they should be; for
The essence to possession is money;
To live comfortably, money is a must.
When our emphasis is based on self-centeredness:
Our luxurious lifestyle,
Our designers' clothing;
Our jewelries and residences
Our business and vehicles;
Insignificant becomes God,
The real purpose of life is ignored.
With stray-away mindset, possessions we abuse.
By such, we end up with nothing.
Flaunt not wealth, status, or position;
To help others, do;

To impress others, do not;
For your possessions are blessings from God.
As God disappear from our lives,
Useless becomes everything no matter how valuable.
For spiritually and morally corrupt we become;
Everything will be lost in a very short period of time.
Examine your attitudes toward wealth and comfort.
Fascinate not on the possessions,
Otherwise, they will possess you.
Your possessions, store with God;
Your focus, eye God;
Your time, spend to serve God;
Your trust, render to God;
And with God, make him your master.
With all the appropriate action,
All will be well and the possessions will be worth having.

LOVE

AFFILIATED QUOTE:

"Mankind is created in the image of God. Since God is love, so mankind should have love in them also. Life without love is worthless; because love is the most important part of mankind's lives. When obstacles knock at your door, love is needed to overcome, since love conquers all fear. For a relationship to be successful, love must be its main core".

Love

Love, mysterious you are.
Sitting abode inwardly in a class by itself.
To love people, to love nature,
And to love new ideas all is what it encompasses.
For to find Higher Power, many things you must love
With liveliness, we wake up the spirit that is part of us.
As part of nature's gift,
An exponent of earth, love is;
An anterior to life, love is;
A consoling matter to satisfaction, love is;
A generator of joy and peace, love is
A mechanism to endure suffering, love is.
For fallacy will faithfulness be without love.
Taken or given, all love is sweet;
Widespread it is as light overshadows darkness;
And with a presence that wearies not;
For selflessly it is given.

Some search for thee in the ocean deep below;
But where are you. Nature it is;
Part of God's given gift it is.
Personal is the feeling; personal is the attitude.
With the pleasure of looking at each other, love is born;
With the necessity of seeing each other, love is fed;
With the happiness implanted in one another, love is developed;
With the impossibility of separation, love is concluded.
With lots of love, obstacles can be faced.
To love we must surrender as it conquers all.
For love you search;
Have you checked the community, friends, and groups?
Have you seek it from Higher Power?
Listen carefully, the way treatment is renders to others,
Donate the care and love of God.
As love makes the world goes around not;
So love is what makes the adventure worthwhile.

You sit there feeling miserable;
All what you think about is your other half;
Have you expressed your feeling?
Love you should execute best.
For the acceptance of nature,
So directed over to love is our life.
Love is respect; love is truth with kindness;
Love is being willing to forgive;
Love is willing to accept and help others;
And love is to perceive how Higher Power wants us to act.
To act ourselves is being lovable;
Allowing others to get to know us is being lovable;
For when others love us, enjoyment is gained.
For allowing others as part of us, is love;
When we feel a special someone inside of us, is love;
With God through spiritual love,
Part of us he becomes.

Love like measles,
Severe not it is the first time it engulfs its victim;
When contacted later in life,
Aggressively it becomes and spread rapidly.
As death is strong, so strong is love;
Neither time, nor disaster can kill it;
Priceless it is,
For it cannot be purchased for a price
Even the wealthiest person alive cannot purchase it.
Like a fire love flashes,
The brightest kind of flame it burns.
Many waters cannot quench it,
Not even the great rivers can drown it.
As a gift to God, it is the greatest of all human qualities;
An attribute of God himself it is.
Enjoy love and share it;
Enjoy the peace generated by love.

Worthless is life without love,
For abandoned you feel;
Lonesome if life without love,
For stressed and depressed you feel;
Over comer of fear love is;

About love, think more
For love expels all fear.
Life with love is a primary objective and ambition;
For it is the most significant part of mankind's lives.
For love and relationship are twins;
Love is life;
Relationship is life;
For it is love, love, and love that conquers fear in relationship.
For with love, you think of each other;
You know you have each other,
Mutually you submit to each other;
Love now flourished in the relationship.

Think not of love as what brings good feeling in romantic session;
For lust it is;
Selfishness and misconception it is;
For God is love;
An action, not a feeling is what real love is all about;
For it produces selfless sacrificial giving.
Real love is like God:
Patient love is;
Holy love is; Unity love is;
Just love is; Kind love is;
Peace love is; Compassionate love is;
Caring love is;
Knowing and understanding God,
Give the true meaning of love.
A durable fire true love becomes;
Continuously it burns in the mind and
Within forever it stays.

Love is more than fancy words;
Commitment and conduct it is;
Based on love your conduct;
With love for God, faithful will your conduct be.
Focus not on yourself;
Think not only of yourself;
A fallacy it is as sin cools your love for God and others.
To real and genuine love beyond politeness and hypocrisy,
God calls us.
Genuine love requires concentration and effort;

It demands time, strength, endurance,
Courage, money, and personal involvement
With genuine love,
Your enemies, you love;
Your enemies, you treat well;
Then, God Almighty will become the Lord of your life.
Now love is saturated all over you.

CONSEQUENCES

AFFILIATED QUOTE:

"Rush not into making a decision or taking an action; carefully
analyze the consequences of any action.
Irresponsible you'll become if you make an intentional
wrongful decision or action that consequently affects you and
others around you.
Be careful in whatever you do. Utilize the turtle steps; utilize
the breathing technique to relax your mind. Pray and ask God
for direction. Then, make a rightful decision or action".

Consequences

Responsibility for our action we must take;
Good is the consequences if in God's path,
When horizontal and parallel we operate.
Tragic is the consequences if in God's path,
When vertical and perpendicular we operate.
Marching onward with God we can choose;
Drifting away in self path we can advance.
The consequence is your choice.
About the plain facts of life,
God renders us compassion, restriction, and warning
To stay away from wrongful and dangerous actions,
God warns us;
In similar manner, children are warned to stay away from
Fire and dangerous places;
Irreversible and severe is the consequences of disobedience.
In his word with love and motivation,
God guides us.
To avoid serious consequences from neglecting his command,
God guides us.
Irresponsible we become with disobedience,
Irresponsible we become with arrogance,
Irresponsible we become with selfishness,
Irresponsible we become with vainglory;
With such attributes, distance away from God we become;
Just like with dangerous toxic garbage,
Irresponsible individuals polluting the rivers and streams;
To the environment and human's health, damage is caused.
Think through possible consequences before acting;
Potential sorrow and suffering can be prevented.

Recklessly decision is made in disregard of consequences.
Now confused and in frenzy,
For the outcome of your action, you start scrapping around;
Darkness now arrived at your doorsteps.
The positive and negative, you must carefully weigh;
The affected parties and consequences, you must consider.
Your decision, rush not;
For thy mind is blinded with ego to get it done.
Be careful, potential problems with negative outcomes may be missed.

Potential consequences you plan and address.
Some wrongful acts may be done in the closet,
Some wrongful acts may be done in the clouds,
Just because you perceive no one will notice.
It doesn't mean some is not aware of the deed.
No, no, no, consciously you should proceed;
You'll discover that quietly,
The wrong act has been breeding serious consequences.
Sometimes a conflict may be unavoidable;
Just like an open warfare,
Heroic and courageous it may seem,
But usually, it is not the best choice.
Sort always an alternative to an action,
Divine counsel, you seek; pray, meditate, and relax;
No matter how hard it is, a solution is on the way.
As systematic God is, into decision, he rushes not.
So like God you become by analyzing before taking action.
As you become enhanced, by deciding carefully,
Unwanted consequences you eliminate.

Turtle steps you now adopt;
Carefully, intensively all variables are analyzed.
Negative and positive consequences,
In decision making are now main core.
Glued into thee is persistence; scraped from thee is stubbornness;
Good, persistence is; self-centered, stubbornness is;
Rebellion toward God is stubbornness toward him.
Rebellion, the grief generator with its accomplice destruction,
Detrimental effect on us and those around us, they may cause.
A sin is rebellion; once a sin is committed, a domino effect it possesses,
That will create a series of consequences that are unwanted.
Bitter may the consequence be and even with repentance.
Remain will some scars be.
Temptation the fertilizer of sin,
Generates consequences that ruin lives,
Strip away privileges and rights,
And destroy relationship.
Disastrous impact in your life and others is the consequence of such sin;
With all temptation, you must act carefully and considerately.
An action we may later regret;
Think preferably and intensively of potential
Consequences before launching an action;

Once expelled, reverse not it is once set action is put into motion.
In all action, question thyself;
What do I expect from other?
Then with no haste in horizontal path,
The decision you make with God's command.
All will be well.

MOTIVES

<u>**AFFILIATED QUOTE:**</u>

"In anything you do, ask yourself, what is my motive?
Refrain from false motives. Do unto others as you want them
do unto you. Avoid mixed-up motives; stay in course with
God's command and purpose".

Motives

They march around preaching and expelling religious quotes;
Deliberate false doctrines and motives they are engulfed with.
False they are like worthless trees that bears no fruits,
No nutritional values.
Be not engulfed with false motives;
Embrace high moral character;
Exhibit good behavior; then,
A good religious person thou become.
Just like healthy trees, consistent they are in the kind of fruits they produce
Instead of doing what is right,
Worried you are about getting caught;
For thy real motive comes to light.
If so worried about getting caught,
In less than honest position probably you are.
A warning it is to do the right thing,
The fear of getting caught has established.
Hypocrites they are,
For appearance only good deed they perform;
Of compassion not, and of other good motive not;
Good the action is, but, hollow the motives are.
Empty is such deed as the only reward is that.
For God, who eye deep into thy heart,
Extends rewards to deeds executed in sincerity and in faith.
Good should thy motives always be;
For in due time, with wrong motives,
Exposed will the hidden motive be,
With the real outcome manifested.

The core of mankind's attitude is self-centered it is
As engulfed in the mind with dishonesty and selfishness.
Of itself, it is aware.
Doing the right thing has become a problem.
Be careful with what thy motives are.
If pure is thy motive,
Afraid not will thou be to request great things from God.
Pre-fix such, examine thy desires;
If existing are any arrogance, selfishness, or self-centeredness

With thy attributes, clear thyself from all;
Then, for wisdom and ability, submit your petition to God.
Sometimes right actions are difficult to discern;
Sometimes doing the right thing we mistakenly think we are;
Help thyself;
First thy motive, you identify;
Then unto God, you submit thy petition.
With such move,
God will be please with your real motives.
Selfish not should thy motives be;
Quietly and secretly should thy good deeds be with
No expectation of rewards.
Thy motives check and execute with generosity and prayer;
Be God-centered, and self-centered not;
For the glory of God, execute thy deeds;
Not to make you look good.
For those who does something not in loving sacrifices.
But to glorify thee, God will disregard.

In giving to God and others,
Pure must thy motives be; avoid mixed motives.
Give not because thou expect benefit in return;
Give with love, compassion, and with the pleasure of giving.
When God wants you to respond in your life,
Look for that rejuvenating spirit; take the initiative;
What God has prescribed, resolve by taking action;
God's will, move out to execute.
Easy it is to eye back thy mistakes,
The foolishness, thou recognize;
Much harder it is to eye ongoing foolish actions which are in motion;
For at that period of blindness,
Appropriate they seem.
Before an action turn into foolish action,
The foolish ideas get rid of them;
The wrong thoughts and motives eliminate them;
In so doing, grief maybe prevented.
All the facts, thou find out first before finalizing
When dealing with people, thy decision.
Assume not that thy motives are wrong;
Even with sound suspicion,

Assume not before analyzing.
Execute actions as your want others to do unto you.
With the appropriate and right motives,
Worry free will thou be;
Smoothly will expected outcomes be;
In God's path you march.

DISCIPLINE: THE ADVICE, WITHIN THE FAMILY
AND IN THE HOUSE OF PRAYER

<u>AFFILIATED QUOTE:</u>

"Discipline is enforced to help someone out of their uncaring attitude. Do not discipline in anger; but do so with love, compassion, and mercy. We must make sure that the punishment is enacted quickly after the offense and that the discipline fits the offense".

Discipline: The advice, within the family and In the House of Prayer

Maybe erroneous;
Maybe intentional; so are offenses of sins.
For both the giver and the receiver, unpleasant punishment is.
Part of discipline it is;
Necessary as part of growth it is;
Important as character development it is;
The realistic intention of discipline, thou must comprehend.
For if thou at a position of correcting others,
For fulfilling thy task, hold not back.
Just and merciful are the key;
With the key, significantly exercised is the
Best interest of the guilty person.
With important principles,
The enforcing of discipline with responsibility you carry out.
Suffix the offense, quickly enact the punishment,
Swift, just, and restrain to reflect the seriousness of the offense.
The punishment, over do not;
The discipline of the offender, preserve.
The punishment, enforce not in anger;
The discipline, temper with love, compassion, and mercy;
Those who should be punished,
Deny not that they deserve punishment.
Lenient thou can be;
Too lenient or not correcting mistakes,
Forbidden it is.
For the discipline must fit the offense.
In all you do, remember, treat others with love and compassion.

Children you raise in a loving God-centered manner,
Easy not is the task of parenting;
For lots of patience it takes;
With children, exasperate them not;
Provoke them to discouragement or anger not;
Reasonably assist them to develop and grow.
With love, treat thy children
In understanding societal and God's expectation,
For vital it is in their development.

So be the purpose of parental discipline.
Feel weary not;
Feel nag not;
Feel scold not;
Feel punish not;
The children give not the luxury to do what they want to do;
On the children give up not;
The loving relationship with them, ruin not;
For with kind and firm correction,
Effective will the discipline be
For learning and development tool it is,
Combined with awareness and God's wisdom;
Teach them self-discipline techniques.
To avert long-range disaster,
Discipline thy children.
No matter what you do,
Friendly with love you stay with thy children;
In God's path you direct them.

In the House of Prayer,
Discipline is a must for flagrant sin among members.
Polarized and paralyzed will the organization
Become with sins left unchecked.
Never should the discipline be vengeful;
Design it should to help bring remedies.
For undisciplined sin has dangerous consequence on the body of God.
Suffix punishment and repentance by a member,
Extended should be forgiveness, acceptance, and comfort.
No matter how good you are;
No matter how much good you have done for others;
No matter how much you have done for God's purpose;
No matter how faithful and obedient you seem;
God, the ultimate judge, disciplines us.
Difficult it is to know when God has been disciplining,
But when you turn back the clock,
You'll realize from what you eye later.
With God's discipline, guilt he may use;
Crises he may use; bad experience he may use;
They are the sign to bring us back to him,
And a sign of deep love it is for us.
Rebel not; refuse not to repent;

Turn away not in anger;
Turn away not in resentment;
Turn away not in embarrassment;
With love, openness, and desire to change and to do better,
God is there, turn to him.

THE FEELING FOR MY QUEEN

AFFILIATED QUOTE:

"Love is a custom-made feeling. It is the spontaneous overflow of powerful feeling from in within. Invincible it is as it thrives throughout inwardly. Accept it as a blessing from God since God is love, so we too must have love in us".

The Feeling for my Queen

My African Queen,
My love for you comes in at my eyes.
That love for you is true;
It is real; it is everlasting;
My true love is a durable fire;
Inwardly within me it is ever burning;
Never sick it is;
Never aging it is;
Never into darkness it is;
Never dead it is; ever-flowing all around it is;
From within itself, never turning;
But directly projected to my Queen,
My African, Queen.
The fruit of my spirit is love;
Joy, gentleness, goodness, and faith,
Saturate this love.
Rear it is; Exclusive it is;
Not in the market it is;
Some perceive money can buy it;
Not-for-sale is the sign.
For only one, the one and only love;
The one with my love that is centerpiece of my heart;
My wife, my mama, my babe, my African Queen.

My African Queen,
Down on my knees I am,
Thanking God for you in my life.
From my eyelids as they glance,
Drip my love for you.
As indicated, From in within,
My love is the spontaneous flow of powerful feelings.
Its origin, generated it is from the emotion of mesmerizing,
Comforting attitudes you expel.
The mere thinking of you
Appeal to my greatest primary affections.
Knowing that you are there for me,
Make me happy as a red rose springs up.
My wife, love conquers all things.
Let us hold each other with coordinated sphere;

Let us also surrender to love.
Sweet is our love;
Common as light it is;
Precious in comforting it is;
Echoes all over,
Is the familiar voice
That brings happiness in my heart;
My African Queen, it is just for you.

MY PERSPECTIVES FOR THE ONE AND ONLY

<u>AFFILIATED QUOTE:</u>

"As the one and only resonates in your mind, it's ever present and everlasting, saturating within all over. An unexplainable consciousness it is, when someone is the one and only to you. It makes you feel good; it makes you feel content; it makes you feel wanted; and it renders a joyous romantic life. Strive for someone to be the one and only to you".

My Perspectives of the One and Only

     My one and only;
The soul of my journey is you;
Perfect it is with my love for you;
To think, it is a booster to my heart;
To feel, it is ecstasy harvested;
And to do is what fertilizes our feeling for each other.
A blessing generated from
Paradise is our love.
To Paradise we journey,
With the knowledge we have that God is love,
So we too must have love in us.
Give me the clear blue sky over my head,
And I will eye you within;
Give me the green turf beneath my feet,
And comfortable will my feet be with the thoughts of you;
Give me a winding road,
And I will see your beautiful face and kisses extended to me.
Now and then I think with eyes close,
Tears drip even though distance away you are.
"Hard it is", exclaimed a screaming voice;
With courage and patience, you will prevail.

     My one and only;
Joy and peace you are to me;
You are my inspiration in becoming productive;
You are my strength to endure calamities;
My satisfaction you are.
In nature, you are like the cylinder,
The sphere and the cone in all my perspectives;
With your absence,
My world will be chaotic and unstable.
From no one comes the thought to love;
Darling by your ways, that love is generated within me;
The rhythm, I keep in our dancing;
The season, amative it is in our relationship,
As we generate time of coupling.
Throughout my body,

My love for you is saturated;
As a burning flame from Paradise,
Is that love by special delivery implanted in me.
By reason blessed by faith,
So blessed, is our love.

TEACHING: THE RIGHT MANNER

<u>AFFILIATED QUOTE:</u>

"Teaching is opening of a closed-eye and nourishing the
conscious mind with valuable contents to enlighten and
expand the thinking faculty for a time to come.
Passing along knowledge from one generation to another is the
main purpose of teaching. For with it, the cycle of life
continues. As with other cores of life, it must be executed
with love, respect, and compassion".

Teaching: the right manner

When the calling pays a visit,
Significant is the venture;
With duties executed faithfully and gracefully,
No matter who gets the credit?
Welcome should the visit be.
Pleasant, simple, and understanding should be the
Teaching with wise words delivered at the right time;
From being trapped in a negative atmosphere,
A negative outcome buster should the teaching be;
The execution of teaching duties,
With love and compassion, it should be.
Teaching, informing, encouraging, and correcting others is a must.
With good teaching, promote quarrels not;
With good teaching, promote foolish arguments not;
For in kind, gentle, patience, and courteous ways,
The truth you expel.
The teaching should be design to eliminate confusion about the truth.
When teaching to people's questions, listen;
With respect, treat others;
With planned strategic maneuver, foolish debates, avoid.
What you hear, you must research;
What you teach, evaluate and verify;
The true message, you should never curtail;
The appropriate contents, you should never contradict;
The meeting of the minds of learners, you must always seek.
No matter how intelligent;
No matter how well learned you are;
With open mind and heart,
To Higher Power you will surrender to teach you the truth about himself.
With love, compassion, and concern for others,
Transformed in the right manner, will your teaching techniques be.
For executed work performed with passion,
Satisfied you'll feel in within.

The responsibility to teach children of God,
Leave not to the House of Prayer;
The home, the House of Faith,
To pass on faith to the next generation, is most effective.
For passing along faith,

The responsibility is a necessity;
As from parents' examples, children learn effectively.
Futile it is to teach holy concepts to others;
Wise and discerning in thy witnessing
Should you be to curtail waste of time.
Shedding light on the darkness on the students,
You become as a lamp.
Like an island unto itself,
Stray not to external refuge;
Teaching as the lamp you grasp unto,
As on the students, you shed continuous light.
To the perspectives, perceptions, and repeated statement,
Your ears you extend;
To your mind, openly available it stays to welcome new ideas;
For when all is incorporated within thyself,
Teaching becomes the art of awakening curiosity
Of ignorant minds with future benefits;
Then, profitable the resources are implanted in thy heart.
Like a train with continuous similar sound,
So be the teaching of children;
Again and again, you repeat the information to them;
Everywhere, you talk to them;
On their forehead,
You emboss the information to remind them;
On all vicinity, write your agenda for them;
The agenda, part of your everyday experience you make;
In all aspects of life,
Diligently you open the children's eyes to comprehend thy agenda.

Others will learn;
You will teach them how;
Instruction you give in how the mind develops in consciousness.
In practice with intelligence, devotion, and maturity,
Distinctive should it be for the advancement
In enhancing principles taught.
Learning capabilities and abilities, should be differentiated;
For each student, significant it is.
Well-planned should be the strategy
To approach and motivate the student to:
Gladly accept the instructions;
Listen to advice;
Accept and love the imposed discipline.
The instructions should be well-constructed;

Prep-time should be assigned to master the content,
Confident should the teacher be to deliver instructions.
By the method of teaching,
So compel will the listener be.
Beyond what is intended to teach, go beyond not;
To questions, be ready;
When one speaks, answer;
To the messages, reply;
To commentaries, respond gracefully and respectfully;
To increase knowledge, research;
For up-to-date awareness, current issues you read;
With honest dedication,
Your effort will build necessary skills;
As teaching is the beginning of enlightenment.
For enlightenment, people must be taught;
For a better world of tomorrow,
The young generation must be taught.
An advanced and civilized place the world has become,
As from one generation to another, knowledge is passed.

TEAMWORK

<u>AFFILIATED QUOTE:</u>

"Together we stand, divided we fall with chaos and instability.
Duties must be distributed in different segments
leading to the same goal.
For work to be done each person must have a clear defined
portion of the work within the group or associates; the
execution must be coordinated.
For religious individuals, spiritual battles require teamwork
between the faithful and God Almighty. Your victory depends
not on your strength or numbers, but on obedience,
humbleness, and commitment to God".

Teamwork

The globe and its inhabitants,
Characterized it is with multiple groups interdependence on one another.
United they stand to form a nation.
Likewise, in community building,
One stone is not a temple or even a wall;
Unless a group of stones are joined together to become one;
Useless will a body part be without being amalgamated with others.
It is easy in an individualistic society to
Forget your interdependence with others.
Remember, when a task is assigned to thee,
Others are also called by God to work with you.
Fruitful will the individual effort be in working together with others.
With mutual aid in preparation,
Far more easily will the task be;
Potential perils may be at thy doorsteps to beset thee,
But with amalgamation,
Easily they can be avoided.
Just like wolves in the animal kingdom;
Hunt they do in pack;
Success they achieved in hunting as a group in providing
Daily needed meals and providing protection over unexpected perils.
Advantageous it is in working as a team;
For strength, endurance, and courage will each team member gain.
For when rejection creeps in,
Teamwork renders to the group support and comfort;
For appropriate moves will be discerned;
Mistakes will be limited;
Thereby generating a counter measure to idleness and
From each team member, active maneuver is encouraged.

"Go along, make disciples in every nation", says the Lord.
Multi-task command it is as it includes:
Nurturing, giving, building, administering,
Healing, teaching that
Require duties with amalgamated effort.
Impossible it is for a sole operator by thyself to undertake all the duties.
As one body, the task can be handled efficiently.
By yourself, overestimate not the tendency of what you can do;
As a group, underestimate not the tendency of what can be done;

Together as one body of God,
The accomplishment will surpass whatever possibility thou dream.
By working together,
Fullness of goals thou express;
By working together,
Fullness of God's purposes thou express;
By working together,
Fullness of organizational and societal purpose thou express.
For the achievement of set objectives and goals,
In the House of Prayer, members must work together.
No, no is it for one individual to do everything;
Religious ministries are team efforts;
Link together by God are members to carry out assigned duties in unity.
Within God's gift bestow upon thee, thou operate;
No superstar exists in the House of Prayer;
As a team, members perform their special duties.
Seek not praise that comes from people,
Seek only God's approval;
For in due course with obedience,
Plentiful is the reward.

To teamwork, be not selfish; for selfishness brings discord.
To the community selfishness brings strain relationship.
By such attitude, good impression thou pose on others,
Self-fulfilling pleasure it generates.
To ego, stir not;
For ego trips over thy own fit and thy own will;
And it kills everything.
Spiritual amalgamation we must;
Love one another we must;
Be one in spirit and purpose we must.
Important agenda is tackled effectively when working together.
Like days of old when oil was the symbol of spiritual
Sphere of life and medicine;
Amalgamated they are;
The physical and spiritual cannot be separated.
With teamwork, problems for thyself and others are cared for;
Effectively they are handled.
With appropriate action,
Demonstrating mankind's purpose and obligation,
Combined with God's purpose, will be accomplished.
To accomplish a goal,

Enacted is teamwork when thou encourage and inspire others.
In the beginning created to work together are man and woman;
Unity of humanity,
The wholeness of human problem, isolated not;
From the beginning, promoted is unity as necessary thing.
Self-fulfilling ego must be eliminated;
Teamwork must be embraced.
Working in unity will become the solution innovator.

THANKFULNESS: THE RIGHT WAY
AFFILIATED QUOTE:

"Every morning when you wake up, thank God for the life he breathes in you daily, his salvation and blessings, and for allowing you to see the day in health and in strength. Before you retire for the night, thank God for the protection and guidance throughout the day and night.
Never forget to say thank you to your spouse and children. For others who made a positive impact in your life, thank them. For all others who helped you in times of trouble, thank them.
Let thankfulness become part of your vocabulary".

Thankfulness: The right way

Thankfulness,
An important suffix core it should be in mankind's life.
The flowers of thankfulness exhibit eight colors:
For the life God breathes into us daily,
Thankful we should be;
For our health and physical condition,
Thankful we should be;
For God's answers to our prayers,
Thankful we should be;
For God's daily provision of our needs,
Thankful we should be;
For God's attributes, wondrous, and miraculous deeds,
Thankful we should be;
For God's guidance for discernments in our life,
Thankful we should be;
For the assigned religious associates in our life,
Thankful we should be;
For our family, thankful we should be.
With time and effort,
Our thanks to God and others we should express.
With time in communication,
To God and others who have helped and blessed us,
We should sincerely express our gratitude.
Someone who bestows a gift upon you, simply say thank you.
For our salvation and faith,
Unto God we are obligated to say thanks for the gift of life.
With joy, praise, and gratitude we reverence God;
As we praise God for material and spiritual blessings,
Thankfulness we express.
Praise God all the time for blessings known and unknown.
Discover now that God's blessings are greatly appreciated.

Thankfulness,
More nutritive than suggestive it is;
For perfect moral sense of mankind's inclusive obligation
To express a simple thank you, the truth it exhibits.
For thy blessing and gratitude,
Do not focus or express thanks only on thanksgiving celebration;
For daily with thy own lips, should gratitude,

Appreciation and thankfulness be expressed.
To the Almighty God,
Thou can never express thankfulness enough;
To thy parents,
Thou can never express thankfulness enough;
To thy friends and colleagues who helped thee,
Thou can never express thankfulness enough;
To thy good leaders,
Thou can never express thankfulness enough;
To all vital people in thy daily life,
Express thy appreciation;
Whatever difference others made in thy life,
Express thankfulness for the impact on thy life;
For thankfulness since the existence of humans,
Is the provenience of expression.
A life changer toward attitude it is;
An integral part of life it is;
And a spring of humbleness, love, positiveness,
Graciousness and appreciation it is.
To thy spouse and children, forget not to express gratitude;
For all the family's daily support and encouragement,
Simply say thank you.
With gratitude and joy,
Express thy appreciation for victory over difficult experiences.

HATRED: THE ADVICE

AFFILIATED QUOTE:

"Hatred, the driven force from the soul, is generated from the blindness of the heart.
Hatred doesn't cease by hatred but by love; for love conquers all. Always watch out for that bitterness that grows within to corrupt you. Be strong, do not allow hatred to develop in your heart; for the unexpected consequence will back-fire against you".

Hatred: The advice

From the heart comes hatred;
With contempt as a joint partner,
Hatred comes not by itself;
From the head, comes contempt.
Interrelated they are; both are actions of feeling,
Beyond human control they spread.
Hatred, will you possess;
Persecution, will you possess;
Rejection, will you possess;
All done for that special stand, executing his purpose,
The right stand, the stand on God's side.
Do not be surprised;
For in a steadfast motion,
Faithfully you proclaim God's message;
Ministering for God you continue.
Due to the desire for God's righteous justice,
Hatred we sometimes have;
Not for personal vengeance, but for the love of God;
The approach is wrong.
Angry you can be at people who dishonor and hate God;
Inappropriate it is to handle the incident by your choice;
As we cannot place God on the passenger's seat,
While avenging God's cause from the driver's seat.
With the love of God, to his command we must comply.
For the battle is not ours; it's God's.
Pray we must for the enemies when justice against evil is sought.
For the haters, God will take care of them.
The bitterness symptom, you ignore not;
From others, you hide not;
Superficial changes in behavior made, it is not enough;
For bitterness, the spring of hatred,
Will regenerate if not completely removed;
Condition beyond hatred, beyond control, beyond imagination
Are the by-products of its existence.

The society saturated with pride, vainglory, hypocrisy,
Envy, malice, selfishness;
All contributors to uncontrolled hatred toward someone
Consider "the wall of threat".

Blindness of the heart they are;
Detrimental to one's life they are;
For no reason of yours, no action of yours,
Someone may hate you.
To those who develop strong hatred due to unpleasant experience,
A fence on their progress, build not.
From receiving God's mercy, shield them not;
For bitterness against someone who has hurt or offend you,
It is like a cancer within you;
If not aggressively treated, will eventually consume you.
Like weeds and long roots,
Hatred and bitterness are accomplices;
In the heart they grow;
In all life, they corrupt;
Not only cancer, but dangerous other contaminants they are;
Poisonous roots they are;
That poisonous root of bitterness
Progresses and multiply as parasites within;
Exist not it should be in the House of Prayer;
Nor in the House of Faith;
Not even in the secular world.
For when left untreated,
Unexpected and unwanted consequences will be generated.
Hatred should be part of your feelings in certain circumstances:
To evil people and their deeds, you hate;
As part of the human race, hate them not;
When others are persecuted or mistreated,
Such evil deeds, you hate;
When there are circumstances of starvation,
Hate that condition.
And with sinful lifestyle, hatred feeling is a must.

THE CONSEQUENCES WHEN ENOUGH IS ENOUGH FOR THE LORD

<u>**AFFILIATED QUOTE:**</u>

"When someone keeps violating God's command, it gets to a point where it is no longer acceptable. The current society is full of sinful and disobedient people. To the Almighty God, they show no respect. However, the Almighty God is slow to get angry. He offers chances for repentance and change of ways. When the Lord acts, his power is beyond human's imagination. He never let the guilty go unpunished and takes revenge on all those who oppose him".

The Consequences When Enough is Enough For The Lord

Enough is enough for the Lord
As materialism saturates life as the main core,
The human consciousness, it contaminates.
Idly they sit around fooling around with each other;
The Great One they equate to mankind;
Distorted are their thoughts;
Though the belief of the
Great One exist as the creator,
To them, just a myth it is.
Their actions are centered on societal values:
Vainglory, greed, selfishness, arrogance, disobedience,
Persecution and awful crimes.
Self-centered it is.
What pleases them, they execute.
In the shadow, they exist in darkness and hopelessness.
Around the corner,
Not distance away at any time is that day of darkness.
That day, that special day;
The hopeless and disobedient folks
Will transform like a human running from a lion,
Only just to confront a bear;
Scrambling to escape from the bear,
Unexpectedly, they are aligned with a wall,
Only to be attacked and bitten by a viper;
To eternal darkness, they fall.
You fool;
With a plumb line, the Lord will test stubborn sinners.
No longer will he ignores their sins.
To a sudden end will the defiant sinners collapsed.
Will any of you be able to stand face to face
With the lord when he appears?
For a blazing fire he will be that refines metal.
Like a refiner of precious metal,
He sits burning away dross.
His faithful servants he will refine like gold;
Once again the faithful will transformed to serve him honestly.

Enough is enough for the Lord
As the privileged ones suppress the disadvantaged,

The poor, and the feeble.
You fat cows, dishonest rich fools you are;
Your possessions you expand with selfish
Dishonest practices in spiteful harmful manner.
The foundation of murder and corruption you have generated;
The entire society, you poisoned.
The rulers, on bribes you have based your decisions;
The devout religiously acclaimed,
The pulpit pimps,
Only for a price you prophesy and proclaim the scripture.
Falsely in psychological manner,
You drain the pockets on innocent believers.
By your own pride, you have been deceived.
How heartless can you be?
Do you think you can fool the Lord?
Do you think because you live in rock fortresses and
Your homes erect on high mountains with the best and
Finest materials, you can hide?
To unimaginable ruin you will be reduced.
Thicket will grow on the heights where your House of Prayer stands.
With hooks in your noses, the Lord will pull you.
Dragged away will every last one of you be like fish on hooks.
Even if you soar as high as the eagle,
Your nest you build among the stars,
The Lord will bring you crashing down.
Through the ruins of your walls,
You will be led.
From your fortresses,
You will be thrown.
From your bunkers, you will be captured.
As you have done to others,
So it will be done to you.
On your heads will all your evil deeds fall back.
Enough is enough for the Lord's Anger has reached its climax.
The virgin has fallen because of their ways.
Their eyes are blocked.
Abandoned are they on the ground with no one to help,
There is no chance for resurrection.
Famines will the Lord send to the world.
Not famine of human necessities but, of the word of the Lord. Staggering
from sea to sea, will people be;
Wondering from boarder to boarder searching
For God's word, will they be.

Finally, all will fall down never again to rise.
Some will try to dig deep to the Abyss,
But the Lord will reach down and pull them up;
Some will climb up into the sky,
But the Lord will bring them down;
Some will hide in the top of the highest mountain,
But the Lord will sniff them out and capture them;
Some will seek refuge in the bottom of the deepest ocean,
But the Lord will send sea serpent after them to bite them.
How awful will it be when the Lord
Sends balls of fire against thee and
Command the enemies' swords to terminate sinners?
Massive will be the destruction.
Help you will seek but there will be none.
The only available option is destruction.
As grain is shaken in a sieve yet not one kernel will be lost,
So sinners will be shaken with complete destruction.
With blood, fire, and columns of smoke,
The Great One strikes.
Dark will the sun become;
Blood red, the moon will become;
Faded, the stars will become;
So concurrent will the Lord's visit be with the great and terrible day.

PEOPLE IN DISARRAY

<u>**AFFILIATED QUOTE:**</u>

"When there are spiritual and moral lawlessness in a society, violence and ecological crisis increase. There are anarchy, chaos, and turmoil. People no longer care about anything. Absent from the minds is God's command. People become involved in all kinds of sinful acts. The messages of the prophets are ignored. The unavoidable punishment from God, they ignore. Changes must be made to avoid God's pending judgment".

People in Disarray

It is the days of darkness;
The days of gloom;
The days of extreme blackness with thick clouds;
The sun and moon grow dark, invisible they become;
The stars no longer shine as the sky appears lonely.
Suddenly, there is a voice, the voice of the Lord;
It roars and shakes the universe.
How awesome will the day of the Lord be with extraordinary
Terrible happenings that even the tiniest of
Creatures cannot survive?
People of pride, people with no conscience;
Conscientiously, for the oppressed,
You twist justice making it a bitter pill for them.
The affluent rich,
Everything you get away with;
The poor and needy are squeezed and wrongly judged;
Like dirt, you treat the righteous;
Some of you go around spreading a propaganda campaign,
Proclaiming there is no existence of Higher Power;
You challenge the Lord to sure himself,
To demonstrate his might.
Well, assure you should be that the Almighty God will purge you.
Your wicked and sinful ways are harmful and immoral.
Helpless people, you trample in the dust;
The oppressed, you shove out of the way;
With the same woman,
Father and son have intimate relationships,
Corrupting the Holy name of God;
You very ones, hate good and love evil;
Cannibalistic you are,
People skins you strip,
Like meat, you chop them for cooking.
Like sheep in pen and a flock in the pasture,
You will be brought together in the valley of decision.

Like lightning, the society declines spiritually and morally.
Absent from people's heart is the command of God.
Lawlessness now is the consciousness of the mind;
With violence and ecological crisis,

The behavior of the people has increased.
Vows are made but, broken and not honored.
There is no faithfulness;
There is no kindness;
There is no compassion.
Theft and robbery, they commit;
Adultery, they commit;
Impotent gods, they worship;
God Almighty, they disrespect;
Idolatry worship flourishes all over.
The wealthy and powerful become treacherous;
Their arrogance increases and never at rest;
Their mouths are open as wide as their grave;
Like death, they are never satisfied;
In their greed, they forcefully and illegally swallow many people;
Like weed, the wickedness of the people overflows.
Multiple waits in the valley of decision,
As they swing their sickle, for the harvest is ripe.
The grapes they tread for the winepress, is full;
The storage vats that store the produce of evil, is overflowed.
When the day arrives,
Like a loaded wagon with sheaves of grain, they will groan.
Wake up people, you are like drunkards;
You weep like brides dressed in black,
The death of their husbands, they mourn.
The day of bitter tears is approaching;
The day of darkness and gloom is approaching;
The day when even the bravest of men will cry out is approaching.
That special day will be saturated with distress and anguish.

Like contaminating diseases, turmoil and frenzy spread;
As the day of the Lord arrive.
When that day is manifested,
The pinnacle of the Lord's house will be the highest of all.
Your hearts, give to the Lord;
With fasting, face him;
With weeping, surrender to him;
With mourning, pray to him.
Your clothes tear not in grief;
Your hearts tear.
Turn away from sinning;
For forgiveness comes only by turning away from sins.
For it is not with mankind, not with nature, not with enemies but,

With the Almighty God you reconcile.
For mercy and compassion is part of his attributes.
Slow to anger he is;
With unfailing love, he is encompassed.
The fastest runners cannot get away from the Lord;
The strongest of nations, will become weak;
The mighty warriors will become incapable of saving themselves.
Like a destroying locust of army,
So is the force of the Lord.
Overwhelming it is;
Dreadful it is;
Unavoidable it will be when God punishes sinners.
With consideration and kindness,
Before his judgment is manifested,
The sovereign Lord reveals his plan to his prophets.
Come back to the Almighty God people;
Cease your worship of evil gods;
Change your ways;
Humbly surrender to the command of God and be obedient.
With rejuvenated attitude,
With open hands, the Almighty God will accept you.

THE DAY OF SPIRITUAL CORRECTNESS

AFFILIATED QUOTE:

"Overwhelmed is the Almighty God with the sinful ways of the people. His anger has reached its climax. No longer will the Almighty God allow the evil and disobedient folks to continue their sinful actions. Unless the people repent and correct their actions, the Lord in his anger, will appear like a raging fire and consume everything on his path".

The Day of Spiritual Correctness

Regenerated I am as I surrender to the sovereign God.
When the sinful and disobedient folks are struck by disaster,
I quietly wait for that special day of the Lord;
For me, joyful will I be;
With confidence I will rejoice,
As from the Lord, my salvation and strength come.
From Heaven,
The Lord will leave his throne to trample the core of earth.
As he marches, under his feet the mountains will dissolve
Into the valley, they flow like wax melting in fire,
Like water, down the hill they flow.
A day of clouds and darkness, will he bring;
A day of ruin and desolation, will he bring;
A day of distress and anguish, will he bring;
A day of bitter tears, will he bring;
The day when dead bodied stink the
Atmosphere and decay the ground, will he bring.
Repent people of earth;
Repent you fools;
Change your ways;
Be not stubborn;
Humbly give yourself to the sovereign God.
For he is compassionate and merciful;
He will not reject you, nor turn you back.
With your humble submission, the Lord will embrace you.
The time to change your lifestyle is now;
The time to repent is now;
For out of time you are running.
With mighty force,
The lord will strike all evildoers from the face of the earth.

The lord despises the arrogance of the people;
Intolerable are your evil ways,
For the boiling point has been reached.
The self-proclaimed untouchables, sorrow waits for you.
Every evil and disobedient folks from the face of the earth,
Will the Lord sweep away.
The wicked, will the Lord reduce to heaps of rubble;
The idol worshippers, will the Lord put to sudden end;

The false prophets, will the Lord cut-off their vision;
For in darkness, they will be covered,
To an end will their prediction be.
Sinners will be trampled under the Lord's feet;
To the depths of the ocean, they will be thrown.
People will eat, but never have enough;
Your hunger will pang and empty will your stomach remain.
Sinful farmers will plant crops, but there will be none to harvest.
For that moment, there will be no food,
No water, no protection, and no escape.
Money you will save, but still not realized
Anything and at the end, nothing it will result to.
Like dew sent by the Lord, you will be;
Like rain falling on the ground, you will be;
None of you can resist;
None of you can restrain the force of the Lord.
Pain will grip sinners like women in childbirth;
In writhe and groan like a woman in labor, you will be.
What will you do when the rage of the Lord
Descends upon you with consuming fire?
The time to reconsider your priorities is now, act now.

The righteous and obedient,
Like lion among animals in the forest, they will be;
Like strong young lions among flocks and goats,
Pouncing and tearing them as they move with no rescuer,
They will be.
To their foes standing strong, they will be;
Their enemies will be wiped out.
The Lord will become a mediator,
Settling disputes between people and nations.
Together again will the Lord people like sheep
In a pen and flock in pasture.
The citadel of God's people,
Will come back to him,
The kingdom of God will be restored.
At peace, nations will be;
No longer will nations fight against nations,
Or people fight against each other.
Flourish everywhere, will peace be;
Everyone will leave in peace, harmony, and prosperity,
The blessing of the Lord they will enjoy without fear.

REV JOHN

The speech of all people will the Lord purify,
Obedient worship of the Lord will be generated.
All proud and arrogant folks will be removed;
Haughtiness in the House of Prayer will be no more;
With rejuvenated attitudes,
Strengthen and humble will the survivors be;
With trust, obedience, and faith in the Lord,
Emboss will they be.
Forever will the sovereign Lord
In every vehicle on earth,
Occupies the driver's seat with his GPS,
Leading and directing devotion in righteousness and faithfulness.
From henceforth, obedience and trustfulness is the world.

www.ingramcontent.com/pod-product-compliance
Lightning Source LLC
Chambersburg PA
CBHW020429130626
46549CB00001B/50